Islamophobia & the Ideological Assault

From the Past to the Present

Volume I:

Understanding the Rise & Decline of Muslim Civilization

مكتبة الثقافة
THAQAFA PRESS

Quinn, Umar.
Islamophobia and the Ideological Assault from the Past to the Present (vol. 1) : How the Onslaught of Foreign Beliefs Led to the Early Decline of Muslim Civilization.
Printed in the United States of America.
First Printing, 2018.
ISBN 978-1-5136384-6-1
1. Nonfiction > Religion > Islam > History
2. Nonfiction > Religion > Islam > Theology

www.SalafiCulture.com

Table of Contents

Arabic Ligatures & Transliteration Guide:

b	=	ب	z	=	ز	f	=	ف
t	=	ت	s	=	س	q	=	ق
th	=	ث	sh	=	ش	k	=	ك
j	=	ج	ṣ	=	ص	l	=	ل
ḥ	=	ح	ḍ	=	ض	m	=	م
kh	=	خ	ṭ	=	ط	n	=	ن
d	=	د	ẓ	=	ظ	h	=	ه
dh	=	ذ	ʻ	=	ع	w	=	و
r	=	ر	gh	=	غ	y	=	ي

Short: **a** = َ ; **i** = ِ ; **u** = ُ

Long: **ā** = ا ; **ī** = ي ; **ū** = و

Diphthong: **ay** = ا ي ; **aw** = ا و

The following appear after the mention of Allah:

(عَزَّوَجَلَّ) ʻazza wa jalla [Allah, Mighty and Majestic]
(تَبَارَكَ وَتَعَالَى) tabāraka wa taʼālā [Allah, Blessed and Exalted]
(سُبْحَانَهُ وَتَعَالَى) subḥanahu wa taʼālā [Allah, glorified and exalted above all imperfection]

The following appear after the mention of the Prophet Muhammad or other Prophets.

(صَلَّى اللَّهُ عَلَيْهِ وَسَلَّمَ) ṣallāllahu ʻalayhi wa sallam [May Allah raise his mention and grant him peace]
(عَلَيْهِمَا السَّلَامُ) ʻalayhimās-salām [peace be upon them - dual]
(عَلَيْهِمُ السَّلَامُ) ʻalayhimus-salām [peace be upon them]

The following appear after the mention of the Ṣaḥāba:

(رَضِيَ ٱللَّهُ عَنْهُ) raḍiyullahu 'anhu [may Allah be pleased with him]

(رَضِيَ ٱللَّهُ عَنْهَا) raḍiyullahu 'anhā [may Allah be pleased with her]

(رَضِيَ ٱللَّهُ عَنْهُمَا) raḍiyallahu 'anhumā [may Allah be pleased with them — dual]

The following appear after the mention of righteous Muslims:

(رَحِمَهُ ٱللَّهُ) raḥimahullah [may Allah show him mercy]

(رَحِمَهُمُ ٱللَّهُ) raḥimahumullah [may Allah show them mercy]

(حَفِظَهُ الله) ḥafiẓahullah [may Allah preserve/protect him]

مُقَدِّمَة

Introduction to Volume One

بِسْمِ اللَّهِ الرَّحْمَٰنِ الرَّحِيمِ

Despite the best efforts of those who would wish otherwise, the attempt to misrepresent and reinterpret Islam only serves to push people of sound nature and intellect closer to it. Shaykh al Islām Ibn Taymiyyah (رَحِمَهُ ٱللَّهُ) said in his voluminous response to a plethora of doubts about Islam penned by an orthodox Christian bishop on Cyprus:

> Since Muḥammad (صَلَّى ٱللَّهُ عَلَيْهِ وَسَلَّمَ) is the finality of the Prophets, there being no Prophet after him — none other to restore the religion anew — then Allah has not ceased establishing the means for the restoration of the religion as required for its preeminence ever since, just as He promised to do in His book. So, by doing so, He shows its attractiveness and praiseworthiness in multiple ways while identifying the evils and harms of disbelief. And from the greatest causes of faith and the religion being preeminent, and of the elucidation of the Messengers' revealed religion is the appearance of their opponents, who are people of unmistakable falsehood...That is because when the truth is denied and opposed with doubts, then Allah establishes clear evidences in its favor — validating the truth and disproving falsehood thereby: manifesting the truth's incontrovertible evidence alongside the falsity of vanquished opposing arguments.[1]

This book endeavors to connect two somewhat different concepts in a broad historical context. The first topic, *Islamophobia*, is generally defined as "the fear, hatred of, or

---

[1] Ibn Taymiyyah. Al Jawāb al-Ṣaḥīḥ 1/84-85.

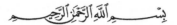

prejudice against, the Islamic religion or Muslims generally," especially when Islam and Muslims are conflated with terrorism and regression. The historical continuum of Islamophobia, dating back to the Crusades, is covered mainly in the second volume of this work. The second broad subject matter is that of *the ideological assault,* which is a reference to the 'othering' of Muslims and the perceived contrariness of Islam in Western thought, in as much as that the Western mind feels compelled to dilute and reinterpret Islam to its own liking and comfortability, attempting to reshape Islam in its own image. It has long viewed it as a threat and wishes to render Islam threat-neutral, not posing any substantial challenge to the foundations of Western thought. Accordingly, it also perceives a need to support voices of 'reform' within the Muslim world, past and present, no matter how volatile those 'reforms' are proven to be or how antithetical they are to Islam itself. The implicit bias in this way of thinking is that Islam — in its earliest original teachings — poses some grave threat to Western thought and its notions of civilization, progress, modernity, and freedom. This is the overarching subject of this work. The foundations of the ideological assault are outlined primarily in Volume I.

In order to fully appreciate the connection between these two topics, we must reach back into the past to better understand the underlying foundations of Western thought as contrasted to the foundations of the Islamic religion. Once we identify the fundamentals of each, we can then determine why certain aberrational interpretations of Islam are more preferable to the Western mind than the original understanding. This insight provides us with a valuable key to unlocking the mysteries of today's rising tide of Islamophobia in Western societies. It also provides us with an important tool for dialogue between the Muslim and the objective non-Muslim who would like to better understand the doctrinal and moral similarities or differences between two markedly divergent systems of thought and belief.

The Ideological Assault

The erudite Muslim scholar, the former grand mufti of Saudi Arabia, 'Abd al 'Aziz bin Baz (died 1420 h./ 1999 CE) (رَحِمَهُ ٱللَّهُ) stated:

> The ideological assault is a contemporary term implying the collective efforts that a nation engages in to overtake another or to cause it to redirect itself towards a specific trajectory. It is more dangerous than military attack because the ideological attack tends towards secrecy and pursuing hidden goals from its inception. Therefore, the attacked nation does not realize it, nor prepare to halt its advance or to stand against it until ultimately falling its prey. Resultantly, this nation becomes diseased in its thinking and feeling, loving what its enemy wants it to love, and hating what its enemy wants it to hate.
>
> It is a fatal disease that devastates nations, removing their identity, authenticity, and fortitude. The nation that is afflicted by it does not feel or realize what has stricken it, making the remedy and the path of guidance out of it substantially difficult. This attack takes place by means of educational and cultural curriculums, as well as through the media, large and small publications and other such means directly related to the affairs of nations. The adversary intends through such things to divert them from their belief and to connect them to what they promote. And we ask Allah for safety and well-being.[2]

The esteemed Salafi scholar Dr. Rabī' b. Hādī 'Umayr al Madkhalī [حَفِظَهُ ٱللَّه] sums up the reality of the ideological assault from the past to the present, saying:

[2] Ibn Bāz. Majmū' Fatāwā wa Rasā'il 'Abd al 'Azīz b. Bāz, vol. 3, p. 338. Originally published in Majallah al Buḥūth al Islāmiyyah, 8th edition, p. 286-293.

The ideological assault from Islam's enemies came early on. Nowadays, people imagine that the ideological assault came to us during this era. Why? Because they don't disapprove of superstitions, innovations, and the denial of (Allah's) Divine Attributes. They don't view that as evil, because these constitute their beliefs. So they imagine that the ideological assault began during this era. Poor souls! Then they come to assault the land of monotheism with their superstitions and innovations. **The ideological assault began before the days of M'amūn — it was in the days of Jahm b. Ṣafwān (78-128 h.). Since that time, the plots against Islam began and the plot was directed at the core of Islam: firstly, (it was aimed at) negation of (Allah's) Names and Attributes, and the rejection of certain beliefs. Ultimately, at the hands of the Ṣufis, the departure from monotheism in worship was carried out.** — These matters led to negating Allah's Names and Attributes and to the denial of many other beliefs. Then, in the end, it led to the rhetoric of the speculative theologians and their alterations of (the meaning of) *Lā ilaha illā Allah* (lit. Nothing deserves worship as a deity except for Allah). The Sufis were affected by that, leading to great corruption, namely, falling into polytheism. By Allah, we go to some lands and see cities built over the graves... Ignorant people don't know about this: cities constructed upon graves... Those propagating political causes see these things and agree with them and they get progressively farther away from the Prophets' call and methodology, farther away from the call to monotheism, which is the center of all revealed religion. They get farther and farther immersed in political skirmishes in the name of Islam.[3]

[3] Taken from the transcription of a lecture titled: Monotheism First; delivered in Dhul Qa'dah 1423 h. Quoted in the book Al Mulakhaṣ al Jamīl fī Bayān Manhaj al-Shaykh Rabī' b. Hādī al Madkhalī fī al-Da'wah wal Jarḥ wal-Ta'dīl.

The stark decline of Muslim civilization was the direct result of the onslaught of foreign ideologies and doctrines that left the Muslims fragmented and increasingly prone to attack. As this work illustrates, these two phenomenon — the decline of Muslim civilization and the spread of false creeds — were not mutually exclusive to each other by any means. The renowned scholar Ibn Qayyim al Jawziyyah (رَحِمَهُ ٱللَّهُ) (died 751 h.) accurately summed up the devastating consequences of the sects eroding the root fundamentals of Islam. He said:

> In summary, the splitting of the people of the previous two scriptures, and the splitting of this nation into seventy-three sects was caused by misinterpretation. The blood of Muslims was only ever shed...because of misinterpretation. The enemies of Islām, such as the philosophers, the *Qirāmiṭah*,[4] the *Bāṭiniyyah*,[5] the *Ismā'iliyyah*,[6] and the *Nuṣayriyyah*,[7] only infiltrated through the door of misinterpretation. **Islām has never been tested with any tribulation except on account of misinterpretation.** Such tribulation transpired either: by way of the misinterpreters themselves; or by way of the unbelievers being unleashed against them. This was on account of what they had perpetrated of misinterpretation, what they opposed of the obvious meaning of revealed religion, and what they had justified of false reasoning.[8]

---

4 A secretive military order who were a sect of the Bāṭiniyyah.

5 Bāṭiniyyah is a blanket term covering many sects of occultist esotericists who, being heavily influenced by Neoplatonism and other offshoots of Ṣabianism, said that religious texts bear two meanings: one being apparent and the other being hidden.

6 An infamous esoteric Bāṭinī Shi'ite sect who believed Musa al Kāẓim to be the twelfth Imām.

7 From the extremist 'Alawiyyah Shi'ite who claimed divinity for 'Alī. Their founder was Muḥammad b. Nuṣayr al Baṣrī (died 270 h.). Ibn Taymiyyah said about the Nuṣayriyyah and the other sects of the bāṭiniyyah that they are more severe in unbelief than the Jews and Christians.

8 Ibn Qayyim al Jawziyyah. 'Ilām al Muwaqi'īn 'an Rabbil 'Alamīn vol. 4, p. 193.

Once the Muslims were substantially fragmented and preoccupied with fighting between themselves over innovated creeds, the unbelievers seized their opportunity to strike. This is a basic yet useful summary of the process that weakened Muslim civilization to no end up until this very day of ours. Shaykh al Islām Ibn Taymiyyah (رحمه الله) stated:

> Those who are familiar with the events of history unanimously agree that the worst sword unsheathed upon the people of the Qiblah (i.e. the Muslims) was from those who ascribed themselves to it; and that the greatest corruption that transpired against the Muslims ascribing to the Qiblah came exclusively from those sects affiliating themselves with them. They are the most extreme in harming the religion and its people.[9]

The following pages provide a brief yet somewhat detailed history of this two-pronged assault of philosophy and mysticism conducted by both internal infiltrators and external foes in misinterpreting and misrepresenting Islam. As we go through the process of tracing the course of history for supporting evidence for this continuum of deviation accompanying devastation for Muslim civilization, we will find Ibn al Qayyim's (رحمه الله) guiding rule to live up to careful scrutiny: **"Islām has never been tested with any tribulation except on account of misinterpretation."** In this regard, Abu-l Faḍl al Hamadānī (رحمه الله) (358-395 h.) rightfully compared the heretical sects to infiltrators who render the homeland vulnerable for outside attack: "The infiltrators open up the fortress (for outside invaders), hence they a greater evil to the Muslims than others who do not wear the garment of Islam."[10]

---

[9] Ibn Taymiyyah. Majmū al Fatāwā vol. 28, p. 479.

[10] Mentioned by Ibn al Jawzī in al Mawḍū'āt vol. 1, p. 50.

The Scope of this Book

The time span covered in this work is rather ambitious, stretching from ancient Egypt and Mesopotamia until today's world; however, the hope is that the reader will be able to connect the dots and recognize the continuum of both the ideological assault and Islamophobia and the larger agenda driving it.

This work is divided into two parts:

This first volume discusses the incremental decline of Muslim civilization due to the gradual onslaught of foreign ideologies, which ultimately resulted in the calamities of the Crusades and Mongol invasions. It discusses how the dual threat of speculative theology and gnostic-mysticism eroded the roots of the tree of faith, making the community of believers prone and vulnerable as a result. A useful comparison between these formative influences in altering both Christianity and Islam is provided for further clarity and emphasis.

Volume II discusses how the same ideologies that precipitated the decline of the Muslim world were the basis of Europe's steady rise from the Renaissance to the Enlightenment. This resulted in Europe imagining that they had discovered the answer to all of mans troubles, leading to the development of the social sciences and their exploitation in the service of empire and colonization. The humanist idealism and utopianism that this tyranny was predicated upon required a simultaneous demonization and dehumanization of the Muslim world.

This phenomenon was a continuation of the anti-Islam narrative tracing back to the first Crusade. This demonization continues until this very day where Islam is conflated with terrorism and regression in the Western imagination, and the Muslim world is generationally nominated for liberation and a civilizing mission ad infinitum.[11]

[11] ad infinitum: again and again in the same way; forever.

Part I: the Foundations of Muslim Culture

Chapter One: Understanding the Rise and Fall of Muslim Civilization

Contrasting The Roots & Fruits of Islamic Culture with those of Modernity

As we compare societies that are constructed upon competing ideologies, then the following guidelines prove to be indispensable. the renowned scholar, 'Abd al-Raḥmān b. Nāṣir al-S'adī (رَحِمَهُ ٱللَّهُ) (died 1376 h.) says:

> Know that the truth and falsehood are at odds with each other, and that good and evil contradict each other. By knowing either of a set of opposites, the attractiveness or hideousness of the other becomes obvious…Whenever you wish to contrast divergent things, then look at (i.) the foundations and principles upon which they are based and built; (ii.) look at their effects, results and the variations of fruits yielded by them. Look at their evidences and proofs by which they are positively affirmed; and look at what they contain and comprise of either rectitude and benefits, or of evils and harms. So once you have looked at these matters with correct understanding and strong intellect, then the matter will become insightfully obvious to you.[12]

In short, he has outlined that the veracity or falsity of belief systems can be easily identified by a simple analysis of its roots and its fruits: firstly, by looking at the validity of its fundamentals, as established by its textual sources and logical proofs; and, secondly, by identifying the beneficial or harmful results yielded by its fundamentals, its sources, and its rationale.

---

[12] Al-Sa'dī. Intiṣār al Ḥaqq.

Know that catch phrases and empty slogans such as 'civilization', 'modernity' and 'progress' have long been assigned as fault-lines between the Muslim world and the 'West' within the Western imagination. In rebuttal of those promoting 'modernity' and westernization who claim that Islam is regressive and backwards, Al-Sa'dī executes the above-mentioned guidelines. He says:

> Severe insistence on 'modern culture' is a matter by which deviant individuals promote their falsehood, claiming that moral character cannot be refined or balanced without it. They extensively praise it and its advocates, while criticizing and mocking those lacking such 'culture.' They explain it in different, deviant ways, with each one of them saying what springs to their mind. If knowledge is chaotic with morality following suit, then this is predictive of how such people will be overall. They will not agree in their theories, work, and morals.
>
> We are unable to fully elaborate on precisely what they say about this misguided sort of culture. However, people of knowledge, keen mindedness, and advanced intellect know that it amounts to a collapse of moral character and a departure away from actual spiritual matters. It stands for vanity, conceitedness, and pride. This is the greatest sickness with which a person can be afflicted.
>
> The only valid culturing and beneficial refinement are, in fact, what the Islamic religion has procured; for assuredly, it is impossible for the self's culturing and for the development of virtue to happen by way of purely material secular sciences and what they produce. The observable world is the most significant witness to that. Despite the evolution and depth of science, it is utterly incapable of rectifying moral character and acquiring virtue, just as it is incapable of lifting people out of vice. The only thing to dependably undertake this

rectification, to assume this genuine refinement, and to direct human thought toward true knowledge, action, goodness, guidance, and rectitude while discouraging it from every evil is what the Islamic religion has brought. It is a rectification for both the exterior and interior, for beliefs, moral character, and actions; it encourages every virtue while discouraging every vice.

The spirit of what the Islamic religion invites to is the belief in the unseen. It consists of belief in Allah the Magnificent and all that He has of Beautiful Names, perfect, lofty Attributes, praiseworthy actions, and perfect control; it also consists of belief in immediate and eventual recompense for righteous and evil deeds, respectively — the details of which are unknowable except through the Messengers. This plants within the heart the desire to perform virtuous acts and good deeds, and a competitiveness to attain the station of excellence in worshipping Allah while imparting goodness to the creation. It also implants a hatred of evil and vice, and it is that which has a tremendous effect in rectifying individuals and society. Allah, describing the believers, said:

﴿وَلَٰكِنَّ اللَّهَ حَبَّبَ إِلَيْكُمُ الْإِيمَانَ وَزَيَّنَهُ فِي قُلُوبِكُمْ وَكَرَّهَ إِلَيْكُمُ الْكُفْرَ وَالْفُسُوقَ وَالْعِصْيَانَ ۚ أُولَٰئِكَ هُمُ الرَّاشِدُونَ﴾

"However Allah has endeared faith to you and beautified it in your hearts while causing you to abhor disbelief, sinfulness, and disobedience. Such persons are the rightly guided ones. It is a favor from Allah and a blessing, and Allah is All-Knowing, All-Wise."[13]

So it directs the entirety of thought, intention, and action toward every goodness while discouraging it from everything harmful; it orders it with justice, imparting kindness to others, and giving to kith and kin—while forbidding lewdness, evil, and oppression against people as regards life, property, reputation,

---

13 Al Ḥujurāt 49: 7

and rights. As for purely material science, then it is dry and does not motivate its learners to be honorable, or discourage them from wickedness and evil. Instead, their inner-selves become purely mechanical—viler than the selves of predatory animals, exclusively working toward their selfish pursuits, whatever those may be.

He then proceeds to succinctly outline the stark difference between the roots and fruits of authentic Islamic culture and those of modernity. He says:

> How significant is the difference between a heart full of belief in Allah, desire for His reward and good-pleasure and fear of His displeasure and punishment, while its moral character is the best and most perfect? This faith and all that results from it has an effect on his self-direction, his guidance of others, and his entire endeavor. So, therefore, his actions are righteous; he was sincere to Allah, fulfilling the rights of His slaves such that he zealously safeguarded his covenants and trusts, being respectful of everyone's rights and all interpersonal dealings. Every person feels at peace about his reliability, his trustworthiness, and his establishment of the rights binding upon him. How significant is the difference between this person and someone who is the complete opposite?
>
> The latter does not have an aorta of faith in his heart, does not desire goodness or fear evil, nor does he abide by covenants and trusts. All who know him and are intimately acquainted with him are not confident about his reliability and trustworthiness; he does not have a fear of Allah to deter him from forbidden matters and treachery. The moral character of such a person has plummeted to the lowest of depths; his confidence and ambition are purely focused upon primping his body and hair, and to beautifying his apparel, appearance, and speech. Behind that facade there is nothing besides shame and ruin owing to what he is insistent upon of traits that corrupt his entire situation and that of those attached to him.

> Between these two types of people is the distance from the heaven to earth. This enormous difference is traceable to whether a person imparts lifeless 'modern culture' or the culture of the religion whose spirit is mercy, justice, fairness, trustworthiness, and loyalty in fulfilling rights.

Having insisted above that Islam be judged on its exceptional virtues, he then cautions the reader against judging Islam, as a religion, based on the conduct and traits typical of the worst of those claiming to be Muslim:

> Therefore, the most excellent favor by which Allah blesses His servant is inner-vision whereby he sees things as they are. So he knows the truth and enacts it while knowing falsehood and abandoning it. Allah alone is the One that guides. Do not look at a person who identifies as Muslim while casting moral character behind his back, using him as an argument against Islam and the Muslims due to his ill-traits, his stagnancy, and his moral corruption. For assuredly, Islam and true Muslims free themselves from someone in such a state even if he calls himself a Muslim — while really possessing nothing of Islam except for a semblance.
>
> For indeed, the Islamic religion is a religion of loftiness, honor, and true advancement. Its teachings, directives, moral character, and deeds all assume the epitome of precision and structure. It has the maximum degree of guidance to every sort of goodness, correctness, and righteousness for whoever abides by it. Everyone knows what the earliest Muslims occupied of completeness and the establishment of all essential worldly and religious facets. They set the excellent standard for human perfection unrivaled by anything else. Whoever wants to know the beautiful effects of the religion, then let him look at them. As for one who wants to reject and delude

others pridefully, then they will have a different outlook than this. Allah's aid alone is sought.[14]

Compare this scholarly synopsis of fundamental, pure Islamic teachings with the invective vitriol of the anti-Muslim narrative and gauge for yourself the intensity of the war of propaganda waged against authentic Islamic fundamentals by vested interests. They have merely taken advantage of the historical continuum of religious and racialist antipathy to dehumanize the Muslims, portraying them as monstrous barbarians: irreconcilably irrational, violent, and licentious. A half-hearted attempt at any cursory and objective reading of authentic Islamic texts and actual history would quickly expose that this default anti-Islam stereotype has been "so radically transformed by time, distance, and cultural mediation that it bears little resemblance to the religion and the culture that it purports to describe."[15]

The Rise and Decline of Muslim Civilization

The French orientalist and psychologist Gustave le Bon (1841-1931) wrote in *The Civilization of the Arabs* (1884):

> Few are the nations who excelled the Arabs in their civility. No people have ever achieved the number of inventions within the shortest time as did the Arabs. In fact, the Arabs established one of the most influential religions which prevailed in the world and whose influence is still more vital than that of any other religion. Politically, they founded one of the most significant states known in history and civilized Europe culturally and morally. Few are the ethnic groups which rose and declined like the Arabs. **No people like the Arabs could**

[14] Excerpted from the short treatise Usūl al-Dīn. Majmū' Muallafāt al-Sa'dī.

[15] Frascetto and Blanks. Western Views of Islam in Medieval and Early Modern Europe, p. 206.

be fit to serve as a living example of the influence of the factors lying behind the foundation, magnificence, and decline of states.[16]

The anti-Islam pundit, Lothrop Stoddard PhD (1883 – 1950) — who was a Harvard alumnus, American historian, eugenics activist, and unabashed klansman — objectively wrote in The New World of Islam (1921):

> For the first three centuries of its existence (circa. 650-1000 CE) the realm of Islam was the most civilized and progressive portion of the world. Studded with splendid cities, gracious mosques, and quiet universities where the wisdom of the ancient world was preserved and appreciated, the Moslem East offered a striking contrast to the Christian West, then sunk in the night of the Dark Ages. However, by the tenth century the Saracenic civilization began to display the unmistakable symptoms of decline. This decline was at first gradual. Down to the terrible disasters of the thirteenth century it still displayed vigor and remained ahead of the Christian West.[17]

What he intends by the decline of Muslim civilization in the tenth century leading to the disasters of the thirteenth is the period of the spread of false doctrines that drastically fragmented Muslim unity and ended with the Crusades and the Mongol invasions. This explanatory model for the decline of Muslim civilization is, at least implicitly, widely recognized.

Contemporary Western historians and social scientists have developed various models of civilizational rise and decline in an attempt to better understand it, to exploit it against their foes, and to prevent similar deterioration in their societies. One of the

---

[16] le Bon, Gustave, La Civilization des Arabes p. 618.

[17] Stoddard. The New World of Islam, pp. 5-6.

most popular and conventional models of civilizational decline sounds something like this one from the late historian, Professor Carroll Quigley of Georgetown University (1910 – 1977):

> Each civilization is born in some inexplicable fashion and, after a slow start, enters a period of vigorous expansion, increasing its size and power, both internally and at the expense of its neighbors, until **gradually a crisis of organization appears. When this crisis has passed and the civilization has been reorganized, it seems somewhat different. Its vigor and morale have weakened**. It becomes stabilized and eventually stagnant. After a Golden Age of peace and prosperity, internal crises again arise. **At this point there appears, for the first time, a moral and physical weakness which raises, also for the first time, questions about the civilization's ability to defend itself against external enemies.** Racked by internal struggles of a social and constitutional character, **weakened by loss of faith in its older ideologies and by the challenge of newer ideas incompatible with its past nature, the civilization grows steadily weaker until it is submerged by outside enemies, and eventually disappears**.[18]

However, Muslim civilization was exceptional in many important ways. It was a departure from the conventional model and must be taken seriously by any people who want to truly succeed and forestall societal disintegration. Most notably, it did not get off to a slow start and nor would it ultimately disappear as was typical of other civilizations. Lothrop Stoddard conceded as much, saying:

> The other great religions won their way slowly, by painful struggle, and finally triumphed with the aid of powerful

[18] Quigley. Tragedy and Hope p. 4

> monarchs converted to the new faith[19]... Not so Islam. Arising in a desert land sparsely inhabited by a nomad race previously undistinguished in the human annals, Islam sallied forth on its great adventure with the slenderest human backing and against the heaviest material odds. Yet Islam triumphed with seemingly miraculous ease, and a couple of generations saw the Fiery Crescent borne victorious from the Pyrenees to the Himalayas and from the deserts of Central Asia to the desserts of Central Africa.[20]

History shows that Islam undeniably declined when it was infiltrated by "newer ideas incompatible with its nature" and antithetical to its original teachings as is found in the conventional model. These "newer ideas" were quite ancient, in fact. Far from disappearing and despite the long-standing political weakness and doctrinal divisions amongst the Muslims, Islam continues to flourish and spread throughout the earth. Gustave Le Bon noted as much:

> Although the Arab civilization perished much like the previous ones, **nothing affected the religion of the Prophet which still has the same influence it had in the past and the same magnificent authority over souls**, although other older religions lose day after day something of their power.[21]

The conventional model for the civilizational rise and decline is the template for contemporary Western thinking on the topic, and mainly ignores other useful, alternative models. One such alternative model of civilizational decline was that of the famous British historian and political scientist Arnold Toynbee — who

---

[19] Such as Christianity, for example. See chapter 3.

[20] Stoddard. The New World of Islam, p. 21.

[21] le Bon, Gustave, La Civilization des Arabes, p. 126.

was likely impacted by the Islamic model of Ibn Khaldūn[22] رَحِمَهُ ٱللَّهُ, whom Toynbee greatly admired and praised. Toynbee outlined that civilizations eroded from within due to moral collapse within the upper echelons of society's elite, who grow nonjudgmental to social evils and ultimately permit vice and immorality until they themselves embody the essence of the depravity normally exclusive to the rabble at the bottom of society. This then permeates all levels of a society until it is irreparably weakened and decays. He labeled this moral crisis "the schism of the soul". Some prominent social scientists have recently redirected attention at the usefulness of Toynbee's model in understanding the current crisis affecting the Western world.[23] Something similar to this model of decline is alluded to in many instances within the Quran.[24]

Whatever the case, the default model mentioned by Quigley places the decline of civilizations squarely and predominantly within the realm of a nation's political organization, a view commonly shared by most contemporary Muslim pseudo-intellectual ideologues of the Western variety. These complicit 'reformers' only assign a cursory, more distant consideration to doctrinal corruption or moral collapse in Muslim society. Their flawed model sloppily fits within the typical modern mindset, as is highlighted throughout this book. **The pervading creed of modernity asserts that societal reformation is procured**

---

[22] A famous Muslim historian who lived between 732-808 h/1332–1406 CE.

[23] Such as the conservative political scientist Charles Murray of the American Enterprise Institute who used it as the premise of his best-selling 2013 book, *Coming apart: The state of white America, 1960-2010*.

[24] There are many examples in the Quran to illustrate this point, such as the one below:
﴿وَمَا أَرْسَلْنَا فِي قَرْيَةٍ مِّن نَّذِيرٍ إِلَّا قَالَ مُتْرَفُوهَا إِنَّا بِمَا أُرْسِلْتُم بِهِ كَافِرُونَ (34) وَقَالُوا نَحْنُ أَكْثَرُ أَمْوَالًا وَأَوْلَادًا وَمَا نَحْنُ بِمُعَذَّبِينَ (35)﴾

"[34.] And We did not send a warner to a township, but those who were given the worldly wealth and luxuries among them said: "We believe not in the (Message) with which you have been sent [35] ". And they say: "We are more in wealth and in children, and we are not going to be punished." [Surah Sab'a: 34-35.]

by human reason adapting and reinterpreting religion in order to reconcile it with individual and civilizational crises. This amounts to ultimately placing Man's fate into his own hands — discounting the extent of the Creator's Guidance and Providence, and dismissing the efficacy of His commandments. Instead of seeing that the cause of true progress and regression is inseparably related to compliance or noncompliance with wise and merciful Divine directives respectively, they venture out on their own into an ocean of confusion. This is actually the formula for all individual and societal devastation as is thoroughly discussed in these two volumes: (1) assigning primacy to human reason over obedient compliance with divine commandments; and (2) discounting the role of the Creator's Providence in human affairs.[25] This is discussed thoroughly at the end of the next chapter.

The reality of the decline and fall of nations is much to the contrary of the conventional model. The source of civilizational collapse is primarily one of faith and belief, with a secondary consideration assigned to moral failure and then a more distant peripheral acknowledgment of socio-political factors. The tree of faith comprises of roots, branches, and fruits. The roots are its beliefs, the branches are the deeds built upon those beliefs, and the fruits are the morals and the good of both lives as a reward for belief and righteous deeds. Beliefs predict moral character and the combination of beliefs and morals predict the longevity of safety and prosperity for society, as these are the primary fruits that they yield. The destruction of the tree of faith, therefore, resides in supplanting and corrupting the Islamic system of belief.

---

[25] Providence: the Creator's divine guidance or care and His sustaining and guiding human destiny. See: (merriam-webster.com).

Recall the statement of Gustave le Bon. "**No people like the Arabs could be fit to serve as a living example of the influence of the factors lying behind the foundation, magnificence, and decline of states.**"[26] So how then did the Muslims procure unprecedented civilizational accomplishment with unparalleled rapidity and longevity? Islam, by merit of its virtues, easily won the broad appeal and support from Muslims and non-Muslim alike as it swiftly progressed throughout the earth.

The contemporary scholar, 'Abd al-Raḥmān b. Nāṣir al-Sa'dī highlights the true force behind the triumph of the truth that allowed Islam to spread against all odds:

> A person is genuinely guided and praiseworthy once they are (1) led to knowledge (of the Islamic religion) and (2) endowed with fear of Allah as well as objectiveness — so that the truth is his purpose — accepting the truth regardless of with who and where it is. Alongside all of that his situation will be complete upon (3) achieving sincerity and (4) following the Sunnah — such that his statements, deeds, activity, and inactivity is sincerely engaged in for Allah's Face, thereby seeking His good-pleasure and pursuing His reward while abiding by the Sunnah of His Prophet. At such a point he will not care about the number of opponents.
>
> He increases in courageousness as his opponents increase because of (1) his knowledge, (2) his fear (of Allah), (3) his sincerity, (4) his following the Prophet's way,

[26] le Bon, Gustave, La Civilization des Arabes p. 618.

and (5) his intimate awareness of the fact that the tallest mountains could not stand their ground against what he has of the truth.

The people of truth do not contend in terms of numerical quantity or material support. Rather, their strength and vantage point is built upon true spiritual strength, the power of faith — the power of truth and all that it dictates of incorporeal reinforcements and then what follows that of material strength. **By way of this, the Ṣaḥāba and the best generations of this nation conquered the hearts with knowledge and faith, while occupying territories with this strength, accompanied by justice and mercy.** They assembled the components of courage by way of their dependence upon the truth and their selflessness. From the completeness of that was their disinterest in false praise. Indeed, whoever assembles these matters, then their bravery comes into full fruition, whereas, if one or all of these matters were to be absent, then (courage) would be missing or deficient.

As for he who does not depend upon the truth, but defends falsehood instead, then how swiftly does he become confused by cowardice and delusions that are birthed out of untruth? When one is not selfless, but instead is in love with their self, then they do not find it insignificant to advance their self for the sake of the truth — which is difficult upon the ego. Whoever fears the blame of the blamers or pauses after receiving commendation, or whoever's endeavor is impeded by the dispraise of critics — then all of these matters are defects that stop the flow of strength and prevent courage.

The genuine person is one who does not care about hardships and only pauses to consider what Allah and the Messenger have praised or dispraised: such are the strong and the brave. Once a person reaches this state, then those that show aversion and disagree will test him, refuting what he says. Once he is sure that he is upon the truth and that what his opponents possess is false, ranging in-between religious innovation, slander, opinions opposing the religion, confusion, or doubts employed to confound people — then this mandates for him to unflinchingly advance the truth, fearing nothing but Allah. [27]

Elsewhere, Al-Sa'dī expounds on the rise and decline of Muslim civilization even further. He explains:

> Look at the state of the Prophet O and what he suffered from the resistance from the people of falsehood. (Look at) how Allah aided him by way of the truth over all of the factions of oppressors despite their wrathfulness, their cooperating to tear him down, and their championing of falsehood. Ultimately he emerged triumphant with the truth which Allah had supported. Allah said:
>
> ﴿وَاذْكُرُوا إِذْ أَنتُمْ قَلِيلٌ مُّسْتَضْعَفُونَ فِي الْأَرْضِ تَخَافُونَ أَن يَتَخَطَّفَكُمُ النَّاسُ فَآوَاكُمْ وَأَيَّدَكُم بِنَصْرِهِ وَرَزَقَكُم مِّنَ الطَّيِّبَاتِ لَعَلَّكُمْ تَشْكُرُونَ (26)﴾
>
> "And remember when you were few and were reckoned weak in the land, and were afraid that men might kidnap you, but He provided a safe place for you, strengthened you with His Help, and provided you with good things so that you might be grateful."[28]

---

[27] Al-Sa'dī. Tawḍīḥ al Kāfiyyah al-Shāfiyyah, pp. 30-31.

[28] Al Anfāl: 26.

Likewise He (سُبْحَانَهُ وَتَعَالَى) said:

﴿إِلَّا تَنصُرُوهُ فَقَدْ نَصَرَهُ اللَّهُ إِذْ أَخْرَجَهُ الَّذِينَ كَفَرُوا ثَانِيَ اثْنَيْنِ إِذْ هُمَا فِي الْغَارِ إِذْ يَقُولُ لِصَاحِبِهِ لَا تَحْزَنْ إِنَّ اللَّهَ مَعَنَا ۖ فَأَنزَلَ اللَّهُ سَكِينَتَهُ عَلَيْهِ وَأَيَّدَهُ بِجُنُودٍ لَّمْ تَرَوْهَا وَجَعَلَ كَلِمَةَ الَّذِينَ كَفَرُوا السُّفْلَىٰ ۗ وَكَلِمَةُ اللَّهِ هِيَ الْعُلْيَا ۗ وَاللَّهُ عَزِيزٌ حَكِيمٌ (40)﴾

"[40.] If you help him (Muhammad صَلَّى اللَّهُ عَلَيْهِ وَسَلَّمَ) not (it does not matter), for Allah did indeed help him when the disbelievers drove him out, the second of two, when they (Muhammad and Abu Bakr) were in the cave, and he () said to his companion (Abu Bakr): "Be not sad (or afraid), surely Allah is with us." Then Allah sent down His Sakinah (calmness, tranquillity, peace, etc.) upon him, and strengthened him with forces (angels) which you saw not, and made the word of those who disbelieved the lowermost, while it was the Word of Allah that became the uppermost, and Allah is All-Mighty, All-Wise."[29]

Furthermore, reflect upon what his rightly guided caliphs, those who accompanied them from the righteous Ṣaḥāba, and the just monarchs who came afterward established. Reflect over how they conquered the hearts with knowledge and faith and how they opened the lands. The truth inseparably accompanied them while Allah's help supported them. Since then, the Islamic religion has been venerably complied with by the earth's inhabitants in the East and in the West. They consented to and accepted it with all that it entailed of the justice, mercy, and goodness that is unavailable elsewhere. Once they slowly but surely faltered in (implementing) this true religion, their might dwindled, and their enemies from every place gained authority over them.[30]

---

[29] Al-Tawbah: 40.

[30] Al-Sa'dī, Usūl al-Dīn, pp. 812-813. Majmū' Mu'allafāt ibn Sa'dī.

Elsewhere Al-Sa'dī further elaborates and contextualizes the rise and decline of the Muslim world along with the current condition of Western societies:

> From the tremendous knowledge of the unseen that the Qurān continuously informs about is that there is no way towards human rectitude and felicity, or for success in this world and the hereafter, except by following this religion and holding fast to its direction and guidance. That is a matter that none can genuinely doubt. For indeed this nation, during the era of the rightly guided caliphs and righteous monarchs — when they were implementing its knowledge, its direction, and its nurturing education for the commoners and the elites — then their worldly life was set aright, as was their religiosity. They became the highest exemplars of power, might, justice, and every other perfection attainable by man.
>
> Later, when they neglected its scholastic and practical guidance, they disintegrated and decayed. They will not cease being immersed in decline, weakness, and humiliation until they return back to their religion. Then, in contrast to that, it is astounding but not strange that despite the contemporary progress of other nations in fascinating industries, miraculous inventions and enormous power, they have not really increased except in misery — to such an extent that their civilization, about which they are conceited and to which others are rendered submissive, is under the constant threat of societal destruction.
>
> All of their politicians and scientists are in a state of great bewilderment as to how to avert this danger. It can only be avoided by following what the Qurān brought and by them pursuing direction from Muḥammad's guidance that comprehensively gathers between knowledge, action, and justice; mercy and wisdom; the greater good of the soul and body; and reformation of matters of religion and this worldly life, and those of the hereafter. That which is exclusively

> materialistic of science and power contains more harm than benefit, and its evil is more than its advantage since it does not have the religion of truth as its premise. Look with your own eyes, you will see wonders. This material progress which the world has not witnessed any precedent for is really regression and collapse because it is devoid of the spirit of religion. The whole world is currently in troubling danger, the extent of whose harms and horrors only Allah (تَبَارَكَ وَتَعَالَى) knows.

This is the true model for the rise and decline of civilization, particularly for that of Islamic civilization. The Islamic model highlights the primacy of sound beliefs accounting for how the religion was meticulously preserved intact throughout the ages. This continued to be so, even as the scholars increasingly became a persecuted minority as false doctrines spread to the masses of the Muslim world. It also accounts for the historical fact that creedal deviations eroded the roots of faith and diminished its fruits more than any other factor.

The Western Tradition of Realizing & Promoting the Greatest Source of Weakness

---

Let us look at how the erroneous model of rise and decline has influenced Western thought pertaining the history of Muslim civilization and, by extension, how they expect the Muslim world to reform itself. The influential American orientalist Wilfred Cantwell Smith wrote in his popular book, Islam in Modern History:

> As others of man's civilizations have done across the centuries, the Arab civilization rose, flourished for a period—and declined. The fall of Baghdad in 1258 (656 h.) marks the formal end of the once tremendously successful Arab empire. The Mongol invasions that (this) fall epitomizes certainly dealt the Arab world a devastating blow. Many millions were killed;

> whole areas were laid utterly waste; and political rule in the centre of the Muslim world passed into the hands of barbarian infidels...The classical period of Islamic history came to an end. This constituted in a sense the first great crisis of Islamic history. Islamic history seemed to have been bogged down. It could be felt that the great endeavor to realize God's purpose was petering out, if it had not actually failed.[31]

He then wrote in an obscure, yet revealing, footnote, "One may note further the not unimportant view that **the onslaught of Greek thought was the real great crisis of classical Islam**." Lothrop Stoddard had also reached a very similar conclusion decades beforehand. He wrote:

> When, however, Islam was accepted by non-Arab peoples, they instinctively interpreted the Prophet's message according to their particular racial tendencies and cultural backgrounds, the result being that primitive Islam was distorted and perverted.[32]

The main trends of foreign interpretation and doctrinal aberration were highlighted by the Oxford and later Harvard orientalist Hamilton A.R. Gibb (1895–1971), the progenitor of Near Eastern studies in the United States. He agreed with the above assessment and further provided some critical background information for the era culminating in the crises of the Crusades and Mongol invasions, resulting in the long-standing decline of Muslim civilization. He says:

> ...from that point on (i.e. after the tenth century passed, meaning the fourth *hijri* century), there were two recognized systems of theology in Islam—the transcendentalist and the

---

[31] 1957 Islam in Modern History Wilfred Cantrell Smith p. 32-33. This book was a long term project funded by the Rockefeller foundation to promote the Modernization and Westernization of Islam and the Muslim World.

[32] The New World of Islam, p. 8.

monist, one that developed to extremes the doctrine of the otherness of God and one that asserted His immanence in every part of nature.[33]

These are the dual threat of philosophy and mysticism that are focused on throughout this first volume. He then notes how this effectively alienated the commoners in society who distrusted philosophy and felt that asceticism was an unattainable standard of piety. The growing preeminence of these heretical sects of mystics and philosophers after the fourth century would so weaken the roots of Islam that its fruits of peace and security would be jeopardized like no time prior to it.

Yet, despite their common observation about what had truly precipitated the decline of Muslim civilization, they still widely celebrate and encourage this bewildering blending of toxic creeds and ideas that polluted the simplicity of original Islam. **The conceit of these Western ideologues in doing so is the assertion that 'primitive' Islam required Westernization by way of Greek philosophy in both its rationalistic and mystic versions to become a viable civilization**. Thus the riddle is solved and the plot thickens.

A prime example of this is found in what the orientalist historian Phillip Hitti wrote on the closing page of the collaborative publication produced for the highly important 1953 *Colloquium on Islamic Culture In Its Relation to The Contemporary World* at Princeton University. He says:

> The three ideas behind the research papers and discussions of this colloquium are: (1) A day had once come in which Islamic culture reached a degree of prestige and progress incomparable in any other language — in between the mid 8th and the early thirteenth century [CE]). It became a viable tool for

[33] Gibb, H.A.R. (1945); Modern trends in Islam; University of Chicago Press.

> transmitting the intricacies of philosophy, the facts of science and the terminologies of the arts. (2) After that era came the era of sterility and degeneration, lasting seven complete centuries. (3) In the beginning of the 19th century, the Muslim world in general, and the Arab (world) in particular, entered a new and vital stage. The result of all of that is that the contemporary Muslim East is on the precipice of serving a new role in its scholastic and academic life that we can call the role of creativity and innovation within the framework of its legacy of religious and ethical values.[34]

In other words, he and his cohorts assert that as Muslims came into contact with Greek thought a century or so after the advent of Islam, they started to become miraculously civilized, upon which Islamic culture served as a temporary vehicle to transmit the wisdom of the ancients to the modern world. After setting that erroneous foundation they assert that after the passage of five centuries their civilization regressed and that this regression lasted for seven long centuries until the age of European colonization. With the advent of the modern era, the Muslims' 'enlightened' Northern neighbors in Western Europe launched a civilizing mission to save them from their social decay and degeneration. The nineteenth century influx of Western ideas during the period of European subjugation and colonization has graciously placed the Muslim world back into a position of **reclaiming its past glory by way of merging Islam and Western thought together**. As ridiculous as this sounds, it is exactly what they have been saying and continue to say in summary.

These orientalists proclaim this as the ideal model for today's world regarding the relations between the West and the Muslim world, accounting for their expectation of how the Muslim world

---

34 Khalfullah, Muḥammad (arabic ed.) Hitti, Phillip (English ed.). Al-Thaqāfah al Islāmiyyah, wal Ḥayah al Mu'āṣirah, p. 582.

is to reform itself from within, as is discussed in the conclusion of this volume. Cuyler Young, the editor of the first Princeton symposium on the Near East two years prior (1951), who was one of Wilfred Cantwell Smith's underlings, commended what his kind had long-credited as being the actual reason for Islam's early progress: the heritage of 'Western thought' common to all Muslims. He writes, **"Together with the Arabs and the Turks, Persians shared the heritage of Greek, or Western thought common to all Islam**."[35]

So what exactly is this glorified heritage of Western thought shared by these disparate ethnicities of Muslim peoples and implicitly credited as being the cause of their progress — in the mind of Cuyler Young and his associates? In their estimation, it was the harmonization of Greek philosophy with Islam! Not to belabor the point, but it is important to reiterate that the historical record shows the truth of Smith's previous admission that, **"the onslaught of Greek thought was the real great crisis of classical Islam**," and that the result of this onslaught was that the original teachings of Islam were "distorted and perverted," as stated above by Stoddard. Here Young excitedly quotes one of his contemporaries and peers, the orientalist historian Phillip Hitti, whose generic model of Islamic history has preceded. He said:

---

[35] Young, Cuyler. Near Eastern Culture and Society. p. 162.

> The harmonization of Greek philosophy with Islam begun by al-Kindi,[36] an Arab, was continued by al-Farabi,[37] a Turk, and completed in the East by ibn-Sina, a Persian . . . who placed the sum total of Greek wisdom codified by his own ingenuity, at the disposal of the educated Muslim world in an intelligible form.[38]

Even more shocking than Wilfred Smith's previous admission as to the real cause of the crisis is his assertion immediately after that as to how the Muslim world was supposedly able to cope with the crisis and forestall civilization collapse. He says that Islam survived this crisis of rapid decline in the 13th century [CE] after the Crusades and Mongol invasions by 'responding creatively' to the challenge in two ways: first, he says, was the proliferation of Sufism which was institutionalized and popularized from that point on, noting that non-Arab Islam is steeped in Sufism. Sufism is, quite frankly, merely an extension of the "onslaught of Greek thought" that Smith admitted was the actual source of this crisis. Specifically, Sufism is rooted in the

---

[36] Abu Yusuf Ya'qub ibn Ishaq Al-Kindi (ca. 800–870 CE) was the first self-identified philosopher in the Arabic tradition. He worked with a group of translators who rendered works of Aristotle, the Neoplatonists, and Greek mathematicians and scientists into Arabic. Al-Kindi's own treatises, many of them epistles addressed to members of the caliphal family, depended heavily on these translations, which included the famous Theology of Aristotle and Book of Causes, Arabic versions of works by Plotinus and Proclus. Al-Kindi's own thought was suffused with Neoplatonism, though his main authority in philosophical matters was Aristotle. (Stanford Encyclopedia of Philosophy https://plato.stanford.edu/entries/al-kindi/)

[37] Abū Naṣr Muḥammad ibn Muḥammad al Fārābī; known in the West as Alpharabius; (c. 872 951) was a renowned philosopher and jurist who wrote in the fields of political philosophy, metaphysics, ethics and logic. In Arabic philosophical tradition, he is known with the honorific "the Second Teacher", after Aristotle being known in the East as "the First Teacher". He is credited with preserving the original Greek texts during the Middle Ages because of his commentaries and treatises, and influencing many prominent philosophers, like Avicenna and Maimonides. (wikipedia)

[38] Philip K. Hitti, History of the Arabs, London, 1949, 4th ed., pp. 371f

very same gnostic mysticism of Neoplatonism[39] that forever altered Christianity, as is discussed in the fourth chapter in this volume. Secondly, he says, Islam converted the conquerors. "If the Arab spirit had spent itself, historical Islam began to flower afresh in Persian and Turkish forms. These forms were different from any previously known..."[40]

In essence, this official narrative asserts that only by doctrinally changing Islam entirely, and by shifting the rulership of Muslims into the hands of uneducated foreign conquerors, Islam survived. How absurd. As the following chapters reveal, this deliberate ideological assault is a cherished tradition stretching in a continuum from antiquity to modernity without pause, until it emerged in full force in our contemporary world.

Chapter Conclusion

The claim of intellectuals and philosophers in any era to hold the solutions for humankind's most significant spiritual and moral problems is both shamelessly pretentious and patently false. What is authentically from the original teachings of Islam has demonstrably worked and continues to do so. The Muslim world was once united in its religious sources, its beliefs, and in its morals, while simultaneously being at the forefront of science, trade and military strength. However, as the genuine progressive, orthodox teachings of Islam were corrupted and supplanted with philosophical hyper-rationalism and gnostic mysticism, the Muslim world fell sick and weak — at which point the fruits of faith diminished, or in specific instances altogether vanished, in

[39] Neoplatonism is a philosophical school of thought following Plato's teachings as interpreted by Plotinus (c. 204/5 – 270 ce). Their doctrine is one of monism (a belief in the oneness of existence, i.e. God, Nature, and Man being of one substance).

[40] Smith (1957) pp. 34-35.

direct response to the erosion of its fundamental source of strength. Ibn al Qayyim (رحمه الله) (died 751 h.) explains the reality of speculative sciences that endeavor to answer the questions that only are only answerable through Islamic teachings:

> Whoever Allah blesses will see truth and falsehood with his heart just as he observes the night and day. He will know that all other books, opinions, and human rationalization range in between: unreliable studies; mere opinions and blind following; false speculations that avail naught against the truth; valid matters without any real benefit for the heart; or valid sciences whose path of attainment has been made perilous — amounting to lengthy disputation about issues of little benefit. Such matters are like lean camel meat on the peak of a dangerous mountain, difficult to scale and undesirable to pursue. As for the finest of what is possessed by the speculative theologians or anyone else, then the *Qurān* contains the same with a more valid establishment and better explanation, whereas, others have nothing except unnaturalness, long-windedness, and unnecessary complication.[41]

As we illustrate throughout this book, the proponents of the anti-Islam discourse — known as Islamophobia today — have long feigned an expropriated expertise and authority on all things Islamic. For over two centuries, they have presented themselves to their constituencies as the Islamic experts. We must adamantly refuse to let them speak on our behalf and diligently resist their efforts to supplant our fundamentals with those of their choosing. Along these lines, the great scholar, 'Abd al-Rahmān al-Sa'dī (رحمه الله) describes their reality:

> So long as hearts are devoid of monotheism and belief in Allah and its good effects, then such people would prove to be the most ignorant, most visionless and most uninformed of people

---

[41] Ighāthat al-Lahfān, Ibn al Qayyim 1/44

about the fundamentals and the secondary tenets of the Islamic religion. You find them writing, speaking, and claiming for themselves to have reached a degree of certainty, knowledge, and education unparalleled by the most senior of Islamic scholars. Concurrently, you find them inept, not even reaching the level of the least student of Islamic knowledge when requested to discuss a single fundamental from the great fundamentals of the religion that none could be ignorant of or to talk about a single ruling pertaining worship, interpersonal transactions or the laws of marriage. So how could any logical person—let alone a believer—trust their statements about the religion? Their speech about the fundamentals of the religion is worthless on principle. If you analyzed the gist of what their figureheads are upon, you'd see that they've busied themselves with the slightest degree of (philological) study of Arabic and had redundantly read papers that agree with their ideology. They have trained themselves to discuss whatever is from the general approach found in these vile, worthless papers. Thus, they and their followers suppose these people to be brimming with information and knowledge, while ultimately, the epitome of what they reached of religious knowledge is merely this.[42]

Today's philosophers masquerading as scientists are no different than those of the past. They fancy themselves as the late inheritors of the philosopher kings dreamed of by Plato and his generation. Overwhelmingly not being believers, yet conceding that religion is indispensable for a functioning society, they aim to secularize religion as a whole. Meaning that they want to remove the concept of God from religion and dissolve it into pantheism, appointing humanism, societal development, and human progress as the God of modernity instead. They suffer from a God-complex, the unmistakable crave to control society, a task for which they deem themselves best suited. They exploit the hopelessness following human tragedies and societal crises to

[42] Intiṣār al Ḥaqq

fragment religious communities and to erode faith and trust in religious belief and institutions, supplanting it with a devout faith in humanity and the social sciences that aim to govern it. As this first part of this work endeavors to demonstrate, the roots of this ideological assault trace back to antiquity. Its proponents have resurfaced throughout history to precipitate crises and then opportunistically position themselves as humanity's saviors.

The foundation of all well being and cohesion in Muslim society and culture rests within the soundness of its religious beliefs and morals. The 'Arabic linguist and renowned literary scholar, Maḥmūd b. Muḥammad Shākir (رحمه الله) said:

> It is a constant wakeful and watchful observer, not lapsing. It restrains the person during each step — in every instance where one crookedly ventures onto the path of injustice. It alerts and awakens him at every wrong turn away from the straight path. **Abstract mental rules could hardly bear such a burden. Rather, beliefs alone are endowed with this authority over Man.** This is because they exist instinctually in one's natural disposition — since coming into being as a sound-minded human — clearly distinct from animals. (Beliefs) can similarly be acquired while retaining the status of being instinctive because one is raised with such things by their parents, family and denomination since infancy until reaching youth and the age of discernment. For this reason, I previously stated that the watchful, controlling principle governing him comes from that direction.
>
> Our predecessors, we Arabs and Muslims, afforded this 'moral foundation' unsurpassed comprehensive care, to a degree unprecedented by any nation, leaving no room for any contemporary or future nation to truly resemble or even approach doing so. **This care for the 'moral foundation' is what has preserved the cohesion and interdependence of Islamic culture over the span of fourteen centuries. This is despite all that has coursed through it of challenges, disasters, and the major events of the times — despite the length of that time, and despite all the weakness it was stricken with and all the deficiency and lapses it was subject to and penetrated with. The survival of this**

cohesion throughout the centuries is truly one of the wonders amongst all the civilizations and cultures which human beings have hereto known.[43]

To better understand the importance of a solid foundation, then it must be known that the religion of Islam consists of the main features and components of a tree: it comprises of roots, branches and fruits. Accordingly, Allah عَزَّوَجَلَّ says in the Qurān:

﴿أَلَمْ تَرَ كَيْفَ ضَرَبَ اللَّهُ مَثَلًا كَلِمَةً طَيِّبَةً كَشَجَرَةٍ طَيِّبَةٍ أَصْلُهَا ثَابِتٌ وَفَرْعُهَا فِي السَّمَاءِ تُؤْتِي أُكُلَهَا كُلَّ حِينٍ بِإِذْنِ رَبِّهَا ۗ وَيَضْرِبُ اللَّهُ الْأَمْثَالَ لِلنَّاسِ لَعَلَّهُمْ يَتَذَكَّرُونَ﴾

"[24.] See you not how Allah sets forth a parable? - A goodly word as a goodly tree, whose root is firmly fixed, and its branches (reach) to the sky (i.e. very high). 25. Giving its fruit at all times, by the Leave of its Lord and Allah sets forth parables for mankind in order that they may remember."[44]

The eminent scholar and Quranic exegete 'Abd al-Raḥmān b. Nāṣir al-Sa'dī (رَحِمَهُ ٱللَّهُ) says in his Tafsīr:

> Then the tree of faith is as such: its root is firmly fixed in the heart of the believer, by way of knowledge and creed; its branches — consisting of goodly speech, righteous deeds, pleasing character traits, and good manners reach into the sky. Statements and actions emerge from the tree of faith, continually ascending to Allah, whereby the believer benefits while benefitting others.[45]

---

43 Shākir, Mahmud. Al-Ṭarīq ilā Thaqāfatinā. Pp. 32-33

44 Surah Ibrāhīm: 24-25

45 Taysīr al Karīm al Rahmān. Al-S'adī, 'Abd al-Rahmān b. Nāṣir. vol. 1, p. 425. Muasasah al-Risālah (1420/2000).

Just as a tree or any plant requires protection from foreign threats and proper nourishment to grow, then likewise is the case with faith. Al Imām Ibn al Qayyim (رَحِمَهُ ٱللَّهُ) (died 751 h.) explains:

> Allah (عَزَّوَجَلَّ) has made the natural course of things as such that beneficial plants and crops are cohabited by weeds and foreign plants of a different species. So long as Allah cares for them, ridding away and uprooting what is harmful, then the plant and crop will grow upright to its fullness, bearing a more abundant, wholesome and pure yield in turn. If He were to leave it alone, then it will soon overcome and overtake the plant and crop, or may weaken its roots — making the fruit it yields of no real value, according to how little or much that occurred. Whoever does not have a first-hand understanding and intimate awareness of this will miss out on great profit without even realizing it. Therefore, the believer is regularly striving toward two things: watering this tree, and clearing away everything harmful surrounding it. By watering it, it survives and remains, and by removing everything harmful from its vicinity, it grows to its fullness.[46]

Identifying the Roots: Belief & Submission

Recognizing the **roots** of the tree of ēmān are essential to better understand the rise and decline of Muslim civilization. Without protecting and nourishing the roots of Islam, then its countless fruits cannot realistically be anticipated. In his short treatise, titled *Usūl al-Dīn* (the Fundamentals of the Religion), 'Abd al-Raḥmān b. Nāṣir al-Sa'dī explains the core root of Imān with the following Qurānic verse:

[46] 'Ilām al Muwaqi'īn 'an Rabbil 'Alamīn p. 134. Dar al Kutub al 'Ilmiyyah Beirut (1411).

﴿ قُولُوا آمَنَّا بِاللَّهِ وَمَا أُنزِلَ إِلَيْنَا وَمَا أُنزِلَ إِلَىٰ إِبْرَاهِيمَ وَإِسْمَاعِيلَ وَإِسْحَاقَ وَيَعْقُوبَ وَالْأَسْبَاطِ وَمَا أُوتِيَ مُوسَىٰ وَعِيسَىٰ وَمَا أُوتِيَ النَّبِيُّونَ مِن رَّبِّهِمْ لَا نُفَرِّقُ بَيْنَ أَحَدٍ مِّنْهُمْ وَنَحْنُ لَهُ مُسْلِمُونَ (136) ﴾

"136. Say (O Muslims), "**We believe** in Allah and that which has been sent down to us and that which has been sent down to Ibrahim (Abraham), Isma'il (Ishmael), Ishaque (Isaac), Ya'qub (Jacob), and to Al-Asbat [the twelve sons of Ya'qub (Jacob)], and that which has been given to Musa (Moses) and 'Iesa (Jesus), and that which has been given to the Prophets from their Lord. We make no distinction between any of them, and **to Him we have submitted** (in Islam)."[47]

Al-Sa'dī (رَحِمَهُ ٱللَّهُ) goes on to explain the inseparable connection between [1] the essential core of faith, which is (a.) belief in the truth accompanied by (b.) compliant submission, [2] the core subject matter of the religion, which is its (a.) creed and (b.) laws, and [3] its fundamental virtues, which are (a) truth and (b.) justice. He says:

> So (Allah) explained (Islam) as being: beliefs and faith in Allah (عَزَّوَجَلَّ) and all that He has of Most Beautiful Names and Lofty Attributes and belief in every Messenger sent by Allah and in every book revealed by Allah upon any of the Messengers. This is especially the case pertaining those named in this noble verse, who are the elite Messengers (عَلَيْهِمُ ٱلسَّلَامُ) sent with the great revealed laws. Also, (He describes it as being) exterior and interior humble subservience and compliance with Allah through obeying Him and obeying His Messengers. And He elucidates that this alone is the guidance and that there is no other way can procure guidance. For this reason, He then says:
>
> ﴿ فَإِنْ آمَنُوا بِمِثْلِ مَا آمَنتُم بِهِ فَقَدِ اهْتَدَوا ﴾

---

47 Al Baqarah: 136

"[137.] So if they believe in the like of that which you believe, then they are rightly guided."[48]

So He elucidated that guidance cannot occur or be incorporated in any other way. As He said:

﴿ قُلْ إِنَّ هُدَى اللَّهِ هُوَ الْهُدَى ﴾

'Say: Certainly the (only) guidance is Allah's guidance."[49]

It is that by which He guided His worshippers upon the tongues of His Messengers; more specifically, it is the tremendous total guidance that Muhammad (ﷺ), the Seal and Leader of all of the Messengers, came with as pertains: knowledge, action, belief, and behavior. It is truth as regards its beneficial information, and it is justice as regards its commandments and prohibitions, as Allah (عَزَّوَجَلَّ) said:

﴿ وَتَمَّتْ كَلِمَتُ رَبِّكَ صِدْقًا وَعَدْلًا ﴾

"[115.] And the Word of your Lord has been fulfilled in truth and in justice."[50]

In the above passage,[51] Al-Sa'dī (رَحِمَهُ ٱللَّٰهُ) has explained that Islam's source texts comprise of two categories of subjects, namely, information (*akhbār*) and laws (*aḥkām*). The information it contains are beliefs that constitute the highest level of truthfulness. The laws that it entails are commandments and prohibitions that represent the highest level of justice. The trueness of sound beliefs demands assent and conviction, while the justice of its simple laws demands submission and compliance.

So based on what is explicitly stated in the Qurān and Sunnah, and elucidated upon in detail throughout the recorded

---

[48] Al Baqarah: 137

[49] Al Baqarah: 120

[50] Al An'ām: 115

[51] Al-Sa'dī. Usūl al-Dīn, pp. 807-808

annals of the creed of the *Salaf,* the scholars of the Prophetic *Sunnah* throughout history have outlined that the roots of faith are belief (*al-taṣdīq*) and submission (*al inqiyād*). **Belief is the statement of the heart and submission is its most fundamental action**. Shaykh al Islām Ibn Taymiyyah رحمه الله says:

> The root of ēmān is the heart's statement and action, meaning: its knowledge about the Creator and its worship of the Creator. The heart is innately receptive to both matters.[52]

As has previously been alluded to and is further elaborated in the next chapter, the foundations of the ideological assault are polytheism and negation of Divine attributes: polytheism ultimately being the end result of mysticism and negation of Divine Attributes being the outcome of speculative theology.

Elsewhere Ibn Taymiyyah (رحمه الله) further expounds upon this point:

> The root of faith is: *qawl al qalb* (the statement of the heart) which is *al-taṣdīq* (credence and ratification); and *'amal al qalb* (the action of the heart) which is *al maḥabbah* (love) in the manner of *al khuḍū'* (humility) — because the souls of the servants have no affinity as complete as their affinity for their Deity who is Allah, the one whom nothing is deserving of worship besides.[53]

Elsewhere, he elaborates even further:

> The root of faith is in the heart, consisting of the statement and the action of the heart which is: **assent accompanied by**

[52] Ibn Taymiyyah. Dar' Ta'āruḍ al 'Aql wal-Naql. vol. 3, p. 137.

[53] Ibn Tayimiyyah. Majmū' al Fatāwā vol. 2, pp. 40-41.

belief, love and compliance.[54] The necessities and requisites of what is in the heart must inexorably manifest onto the limbs. When these necessities and requisites are not acted upon, this shows either the absence or weakness of (the root). As such, the external actions are necessitated and required by the faith in the heart. They are an affirmation of the veracity of what is in the heart, as well as a proof and testimony of it. They are a branch and component of faith's absoluteness.[55]

Ibn al Qayyim (رَحِمَهُ ٱللَّهُ) shows how these components of faith are understood from the consensus of the Salaf that ēmān comprises of statement and action. He says:

> Here we have another principle, which is the reality of faith comprising statement and action. The statement is of two types: (1) the heart's statement, which is al-taṣdīq (belief); and the (2) tongue's attestation, which is to utter the statement of Islam. Its action is of two types: (1) the action of the heart, which is its intention and sincerity; and (2) the action of the limbs. When these four are absent, then ēmān in its entirety is absent. If the heart's belief is missing, then the other components do not avail. For indeed, the heart's affirmation (as opposed to knowing the truth without confirming it) is a condition of belief and for that being of any benefit. When the action of the heart is missing while believing in the truth, then this is where the battle between the *Murji'ah* and Ahl al-Sunnah occurs. Ahl al-Sunnah are unequivocal about ēmān's departure (i.e., that one is an unbeliever if the heart is totally missing loving compliance), and that affirmation does not benefit when accompanied by the negation of the heart's action, which is its love and submission. Similarly, it did not avail Iblīs, Pharaoh, and his people, the Jews, or the polytheists who believed in the trueness of the Prophet (عَلَيْهِ ٱلصَّلَاةُ وَٱلسَّلَامُ). The (latter) admitted it

54 The statement of the heart is acceptance and belief, while the action of the heart is love and compliance.

55 Ibn Taymiyyah. Kitāb al Imān, and Majmū' al Fatāwā vol. 7, p. 644.

inwardly and outwardly, saying that he is not a liar, yet we do not follow him or believe in him... For undoubtedly ēmān is not merely affirmation, as was previously explained, but it is only such affirmation that necessitates obedience and submission. In the same way, guidance is not just knowing the truth and having clarity about it, instead, it is recognizing it in a manner that necessitates following it and acting according to its requirements.[56]

This was explained centuries before by the great scholar of ḥadīth, Al Ḥāfiẓ Ibn Mandah (رَحِمَهُ ٱللَّهُ) (310-395 h.), who says in Kitāb al Imān:

> Emān consists of all acts of obedience as carried out by the heart and by the rest of the body; however, it has that which constitutes a root and that which is a branch. Its root is: knowing Allah, affirmation of Him and of all that has come from him with the heart and tongue; along with humility for Him, loving Him, and fear and reverence for Him; (this is) accompanied by abstention from arrogance, objection, and stubborn opposition. Once a person procures this root, he enters within ēmān and its title, and its rulings apply to him. However, he does not complete (faith) until he produces its branches. Its branches are the obligations upon him, or (you could say) it is abiding by the (religious) duties and avoidance of forbidden things.[57]

Ibn Taymiyyah (رَحِمَهُ ٱللَّهُ) elaborates further:

> As for the believer — who believes in Allah with both his heart and his limbs, then his ēmān gathers between both the knowledge of his heart and his heart's state: the assent of the

---

[56] Al-Ṣalah wa hukm tārikihā, p. 56. Maktabah al-Thaqāfa, Madinah, KSA.

57 Kitāb al Imān, p. 331. Muasasah al-Risālah, Beirut 2nd edition, (1406). Taḥqīq Ali b. Nāṣir al Faqīhī.

heart and the heart's submissiveness, while also gathering between the statement of his tongue and the actions of his limbs. Since the root of faith is that which exists in the heart — or rather it is that which exists within the heart and upon the tongue — (meaning) that he must necessarily believe in Allah and submit to him. This (i.e., belief in Allah) is the heart's statement, and that (i.e., submission) is the heart's action which is assenting to Allah. **Knowledge precedes implementation, perception precedes motion, belief precedes submission, and awareness precedes love — although each is inseparable from the other.** However, the heart's knowledge necessitates its action so long as there is not a preponderant interference; its action requires its (prior) assent since there is no voluntary movement or love except that it emanates from perception. However, there may be some corruption in its activity and love if one's perception and sense are incorrect.[58]

Most of this book elucidates on the consequences of deviating away from the true root of faith. Specifically, we discuss how speculative theology compromises the heart's belief, while ascetic mysticism compromises the heart's love and compliance. The devastation inherent in philosophy and Ṣufism is at the core of the ideological assault throughout history. The ancient precedence for speculative theology and mysticism predating the advent of Islam in Arabia are also highlighted in great detail to further illustrate this point.

The Roots, the Branches, & the Fruits of Faith

As has preceded, the religion consists of roots, branches, and fruits, and each of these are dependent on each other. To fully appreciate the Islamic model of civilizational rise and decline, we

58 Ibn Taymiyyah. Majmū' al Fatāwā, Vol. 2, p. 382.

must understand the particulars of each of these components. In his book *Al Qawā'id al Ḥisān*, 'Abd al-Raḥmān al-Sa'dī رَحِمَهُ ٱللَّهُ succinctly summarizes the roots, branches and fruits of the tree of faith in much greater detail. He says:

> Allah, in His book, has described the believer as affirming and conceding to all of the religion's beliefs, wanting what Allah loves and is pleased with, acting in accordance to what Allah loves and is pleased with, and abandoning all acts of disobedience. He hastens to repent from anything that he committed of that and his faith has impacted his character, statements, and actions in the most wholesome way.

What Al-Sa'dī (رَحِمَهُ ٱللَّهُ) has described so-far is the framework upon which everything in the religion is structured. Al-Sa'dī (رَحِمَهُ ٱللَّهُ) continues, highlighting the core fundamental of Islamic beliefs and its effects on the the believer's heart and behavior, saying:

> So He described the believers as believing in the comprehensive fundamentals, namely: belief in Allah, His angels, His scriptures, His messengers, the Last Day, and in predestination of what is good and bad; they believe in all that was brought by every Messenger; and they believe in the unseen. He described them as listening and obeying, as well complying outwardly and inwardly. He described them as follows:
>
> ﴿الَّذِينَ إِذَا ذُكِرَ اللَّهُ وَجِلَتْ قُلُوبُهُمْ وَإِذَا تُلِيَتْ عَلَيْهِمْ آيَاتُهُ زَادَتْهُمْ إِيمَانًا وَعَلَى
> رَبِّهِمْ يَتَوَكَّلُونَ * الَّذِينَ يُقِيمُونَ الصَّلَاةَ وَمِمَّا رَزَقْنَاهُمْ يُنْفِقُونَ * أُولَئِكَ هُمُ
> الْمُؤْمِنُونَ حَقًّا﴾
>
> "[2.] (They are) those who, when Allah is mentioned, feel a fear in their hearts and when His Verses (this Qur'an) are recited unto them, they (i.e. the Verses) increase their Faith; and they put their trust in their Lord (Alone); [3.] Who perform As-Salat (Iqamat-as-Salat) and spend out of that We have provided them. 4. It is they who are the believers in truth."[59]

---

[59] Al Anfāl: 2-4

> He described them as having skin that trembles, eyes that flood with tears, and hearts that soften and find tranquility with Allah's verses and mention. They give what they give with trembling hearts because they are sure to return to their Lord. He described them as observing humble veneration in their general affairs, and as especially adopting it during prayer. They shun idle speech. They attend to purification (of both their wealth and hearts). They preserve their chastity from anything except for their wives and right-hand possessions. They abide by their testimonies and are mindful of their trusts and covenants.
>
> He described them as having perfect certainty without any doubt and as striving with their wealth and lives in Allah's path. He described them as having sincerity for their Lord in all that they give and withhold. He described them as loving the believers; praying for their believing brothers who came before them and come after them; striving diligently to remove hatred from their hearts toward the believers; having allegiance to Allah and the Messenger (صَلَّى ٱللَّٰهُ عَلَيْهِ وَسَلَّمَ), and to Allah's believing worshippers. They disassociate from the religion's foes and they command with goodness while forbidding evil. They obey Allah and the Messenger (صَلَّى ٱللَّٰهُ عَلَيْهِ وَسَلَّمَ) in every circumstance.
>
> So Allah gathered within the (believers) true beliefs, total certainty and the perfect practice of regularly turning (to Him). This results in their complying by implementing commandments, abstaining from forbidden matters, and stopping short from exceeding the religion's parameters.

So far, Al-Sa'dī (رَحِمَهُ ٱللَّٰهُ) has outlined the roots and the branches of faith. He then continues, elucidating on the fruits yielded by the tree of faith. He says:

> These noble qualities are the description of the absolute believer who is safe from punishment and deserving of reward,

who attains every good resulting from faith. For assuredly, Allah, in His book, has designated benefits and fruits related to ēmān that are no fewer than one hundred benefits in number. Each one of them is better than the world and all that it contains.

He has made attainment of His good-pleasure, which surpasses everything, to result from faith. Also, He has also made the following matters to emerge from faith: entrance into paradise; salvation from hell-fire; security from the punishment of the grave, from the difficulties of Judgment Day, and from their affairs falling into disarray. They will have perfect glad-tidings in this life and in the Hereafter, and they will have resoluteness upon faith and obedience in this world, at the time of death. They will have it in the grave by having faith and tawḥīd and through the beneficial correct response (to the questions of the angels). Also, as a result of faith, He has facilitated for them a wholesome life, sustenance, goodness, and ultimate ease in this world. They will be made distant from extreme hardship. They will have repose in their hearts, relaxation of the soul and total satisfaction. They will experience rightness in their overall condition and with their offspring, who will be the coolness of the believer's eye. They will enjoy patience during tribulations and calamities, Allah's removal of their burdens, Allah's defending them against all evils, and triumph against the enemy. They will have an excuse from any accountability due to being forgetful, ignorant, and being mistaken. Allah has removed the previous hardships and shackles (imposed upon earlier nations) and has not made them bear more than they are able. Because of faith, He forgives them of their sins and guides them to repentance.

Therefore faith is the most significant means of nearness to Allah and His mercy, as well as attainment of His reward. It is the most excellent means of forgiveness of sins and for the removal and alleviation of all hardships. In detail, the fruits of faith are many, yet in summary, all of the good in this world and

> the hereafter result from ēmān, just as all evils result from an absence thereof. And Allah knows best.[60]

In the above passage, this renowned scholar has summarized most of what occurs in the Qurān pertaining the roots, branches, and fruits of faith. This diagram provides us with the Islamic methodology of reformation and civilizational progress. To yield the fruits of faith, then the foundation and structure of this tree must be protected and nourished.

Reinforcing the Foundation of Faith

In addition to what has preceded, Ibn al Qayyim رَحِمَهُ ٱللَّهُ explains the inseparability and interrelatedness of the interior and exterior dimensions of faith. He says:

> Principle: Emān has an exterior and an interior. Its exterior consists of the statement of the tongue and action of the limbs. Its interior is the affirmation of the heart, as well as its submission and love. An exterior without an interior does not benefit... An interior with no exterior does not avail except when that is not possible due to inability, compulsion, or fear of demise. Externally withholding from implementation without there being any hindrance, is a proof of the corruption of one's interior and its vacancy of faith. A deficiency (in action) is a proof of an insufficiency (in faith), and its strength is a proof of its strength. Faith is the heart and core of Islam and certainty is the heart and root of faith. Any knowledge and action that does not increase one's faith and certainty are contaminated, and any faith that does not drive one to action is contaminated.[61]

---

60 Al Qawā'id al Ḥisān

61 Ibn al Qayyim. Al Fawā'id, p. 85-86.

Elsewhere, he thoroughly outlines the importance of understanding the particulars of belief and compliance as relates the actions built upon it and the fruit that it yields. He says (رَحِمَهُ ٱللَّٰهُ):

> Whoever wants his building to stand tall, must first make its foundation dependable and well-constructed, and must afford maximum care in doing so: for indeed the highness of the structure is entirely dependent on how dependable and well-constructed the foundation is made. Therefore, good deeds and high degrees of virtue are a building whose foundation is faith. So long as the foundation is made dependable, it will bear the building, which will stand tall upon it, and if anything of the building then crumbles, it will be simple to repair.
>
> However, if the foundation has not been made dependable, the building will not stand tall, nor will it be stable. If something of the foundation then collapses, then the building will fall, or it will nearly do so. The ambition of a person who has deep understanding is therefore to correct the foundation and to be meticulous in doing so, whereas the ignoramus builds up high without any foundation, so his building will not remain for long until it falls.
>
> The foundation for the structure of deeds is like strength to the human body. So long as one has adequate strength, then it will carry the body while warding off many maladies. When one's health is weak, its ability to bear the body will be impaired, and illnesses will quickly rush towards it. So carry your body upon the strength of faith, so that if anything from the top and roof of the structure falls into disrepair, it will be easy to repair as opposed to damage to the foundation.
>
> This foundation consists of two matters: **correct awareness about Allah, His names, and His attributes; second, pure devotion of one's compliance for Him and His Messenger (صَلَّى ٱللَّٰهُ عَلَيْهِ وَسَلَّمَ) to the exclusion of all else.** This is

the most unbreakable foundation upon which the worshipful slave can construct his building. Accordingly, he can then build as high as he would like.[62]

The Ark of Salvation: Navigating through What is Predestined by Complying with Divine Commandment

As is explained in what follows, just as the core of the religion is faith and submission, then the most devastating thing to one's religion is (1) to lose faith in Allah's Authority and Providence over the creation and (2) to refrain from compliance with His commandments. Correct beliefs about and worship of the Creator is the purpose of life, resulting in true felicity and well-being. It is the core of the message of the Prophets (عَلَيْهِمُ السَّلَامُ). This foundation has been revealed in order to stabilize people and to direct them towards the best outcomes of cause and effect within His preordainments in this world. Ibn al Qayyim (رَحِمَهُ ٱللَّهُ) explains a parable for this in many places. He likens Allah's testing humanity in this world to an ocean. The ark of salvation required to survive the storms of life represents compliance with the Creator's commandments. . He says (رَحِمَهُ ٱللَّهُ):

> The parable of (the world) is like the sea which all of creation must sail across to pass onto the shores containing their abodes, their homelands, and their settlement. It is only possible to cross it in an ark of salvation. So Allah (تَبَارَكَ وَتَعَالَىٰ) sent His Messengers (عَلَيْهِمُ السَّلَامُ) to teach the nations how to utilize arks of salvation, commanding them to construct and sail upon them. These (arks) comprise of obedience to Him, obedience to His Messengers, worshipping Him, devoting actions sincerely to Him, and diligently striving towards, desiring, and racing towards the Hereafter. Those who are divinely guided advanced, sailing upon the arks, being disinterested in diving

[62] Ibn Qayyim al Jawziyyah. Al Fawā'id. 155-156.

into the ocean out of knowing that diving in or swimming across will not suffice to be able to cross it. As for the stupid ones, then they deemed it too difficult to construct the ships and the tools to do so, as well as sailing upon them. They said: we will dive into the ocean, and if we become overpowered we will try to swim. They are the majority of the people of this world. So they plunged in, and when they became unable to wade, they attempted swimming until they were ultimately overcome by drowning, whereas the people on the ark survived, just as Noah (عَلَيْهِ الصَّلَاةُ وَالسَّلَامُ) survived while the people of the earth perished. Reflect on this parable and the state of the people in this world — and its conformity to reality will become abundantly clear to you.[63]

In similar fashion, in the introduction of his voluminous *Sharḥ Usūl 'Itiqād Ahlis-Sunnah wal Jama'āh,*[64] the great scholar, Abul Qāsim Hibatullah b. Al Ḥasan al-Lālakā'ī (رَحِمَهُ ٱللَّهُ) (died 418 h.) describes this path of salvation and its alternative as a matter of: (1.) giving precedence to the revealed texts over human reasoning and (2.) believing in the supremacy of Divine Providence in regulating human affairs. He says:

> Whoever adopts such a path and maintains usage of these proofs upon the methodology of the *sharī'ah* will be safe from blame in his religion in both an immediate and an ultimate sense. He will have grasped the firmest handhold that is unbreakable. He will have protected himself with a shield of superior protection — fortifying himself by way of these things and hastening their blessing. He will, in turn, have a praiseworthy outcome thereby in his ultimate return and final abode — Allah willing.

---

[63] 'Idah al-Ṣābirīn p. 236

[64] Explanation of the Fundamentals if the Creed of the Adherents to the Sunnah and Unity.

> Whoever turns away in aversion, seeking the truth elsewhere from whatever he fancies, or aims for some alternative beyond it, has erred in choosing his objective and has been set astray thereby. It will lead him into the path of misguidance, causing him to perish in the abysses of destruction due to: disagreeing with Allah's Book and the Sunnah of His Messenger صَلَّى ٱللَّهُ عَلَيْهِ وَسَلَّمَ by proposing similitudes; rejecting them with a variety of impossible conclusions; departing from it because of hearsay — which Allah تَبَارَكَ وَتَعَالَىٰ has revealed no authority for. (He will) adopt what the people of exegesis and language are unfamiliar with and what the heart of no intelligent person could imagine an argument to dictate — that which the heart of no monotheist could feel comfortable with after its contemplation and witnessing. The *Shayṭān* has overtaken him, and a forsaken state envelops him. He has gone astray by disobedience to Al-Raḥmān until he deluded himself with lying and falsehood.

After outlining this preliminary point about compliance with the texts being the true path of salvation, whereas following the whimsicalities of human reason accounts for the path of damnation, Al-Lālakā'ī (رَحِمَهُ ٱللَّهُ) goes on to explain a most crucial point. He identifies the cause of this historic conflict between faith and reason as being the direct result of questioning Divine Providence and the suitability of revealed religion to respond to crisis and challenges in the world. He describes this as being the volatile concoction of the earliest speculative theologians whom the scholars of Islam publicly warned the masses about:

> So he is constantly in thought about the Providence of Allah's Kingdom with his defeated mind and inverted understanding. He disapproves of what he imagines as unbecoming and approves of what he imagines as good, or he attributes oppression and foolishness (to predestiny) without insight. He may declare as fair whatever might momentarily occur to his imagination, or deem as oppressive whatever his Shayṭān whispers to him. Owing to his terrible ignorance, he declares

the impossibility of (Allah's) creating the actions of His servants, or mandates upon (Allah) incumbent rights towards His servants — deeming this to be binding on Him. There are no rights **binding** on Allah (جَلَّ وَعَلَا), but rather He is the one to Whom binding rights and mandatory duties are due from His servants and He is the one who bountifully gives to them out of His generosity and kindness.

Had only he returned the origin of matters to Him and saw that their preordainment came from Him — assigning Him Divine Will as pertains His Dominion and Authority and not appointing another Creator besides Him. Had only he just submitted to Him, then he would have been spared from associationism and objecting to Him. This person is running around day and night refuting Allah's Book and the Sunnah of His Messenger, while abusively criticizing them both. He disputes about them both with farfetched misinterpretations, or he assigns authority to his doubtful opinionating against whatever does not agree with his weak, manufactured doctrine until forcing the Book and the Sunnah into compliance. And how could they ever conform?

Had only he taken the path of the believers, and followed the way of the real followers, then he would have built his doctrine upon the (Qurān and Sunnah) and followed their lead. However, he is obstructed and diverted from goodness. Since he energetically disputes about the Book and Sunnah, then this is his condition.[65]

Elsewhere, Ibn al Qayyim (رَحِمَهُ ٱللَّهُ) explains how questioning Allah's orders and doubting His Control over the universe constitutes the foundation of all of Man's deviation. He says:

As regards being tested, the creation split into two groups:

[65] *Sharḥ Usūl 'Itiqād Ahlis-Sunnah wal Jama'āh.* Abul Qāsim Hibatullah b. Al Ḥasan al-Lālakā'ī (died 418 h.) p. 8-10.

One group centered itself around His commandments and what He loves. They stopped where the orders halted them and moved wherever the commandments moved them. They employed the commandments pertaining (reacting to) preordainment. They sailed upon the ark of divine commandment within the ocean of predestiny. They countered destiny with destiny by enacting His commandments and pursuing His good pleasure. These alone are saved.

The second group asserted that there is a contradiction between the commandments and the preordainments — between what He loves and is pleased with and what He predestined and preordained.

Then Ibn al Qayyim رَحِمَهُ ٱللَّهُ elaborates in detail the different major erroneous approaches mankind has taken pertaining the belief in *al qadar*, fragmenting into many schisms and sects as a result of deviation in this matter of creed. He concludes:

All of these sects follow *Iblīs*, their chieftain. He was the first to assign primacy to fate over (revealed) commandment and counterpoise it with it. He said:

﴿ قَالَ رَبِّ بِمَا أَغْوَيْتَنِي لَأُزَيِّنَنَّ لَهُمْ فِي الْأَرْضِ وَلَأُغْوِيَنَّهُمْ أَجْمَعِينَ ﴾

"[Iblis (Satan)] said: "O my Lord! Because you misled me, I shall indeed adorn the path of error for them (mankind) on the earth, and I shall mislead them all."[66]

﴿ قَالَ فَبِمَا أَغْوَيْتَنِي لَأَقْعُدَنَّ لَهُمْ صِرَاطَكَ الْمُسْتَقِيمَ ﴾

"(Iblis) said: "Because You have sent me astray, surely I will sit in wait against them (human beings) on Your Straight Path."[67]

He rejected Allah's commandment by using His *Qadar* (as an argument) — he used predestiny as an argument against his Lord, and then his acolytes split into four sects, as you have

---

[66] Al Ḥijr: 39

[67] Al 'Arāf: 16

seen. So Iblīs and his legions have been dispatched (as a test) with fate by preordainment, such that fate is their religion. Allah تَبَارَكَ وَتَعَالَى said:

﴿ أَلَمْ تَرَ أَنَّا أَرْسَلْنَا الشَّيَاطِينَ عَلَى الْكَافِرِينَ تَؤُزُّهُمْ أَزًّا ﴾

"See you not that We have sent the Shayatin (devils) against the disbelievers to push them to do evil."[68]

Their religion is fate, and their destination is a blazing fire. So Allah sent the Messengers with the commandments, ordering them to combat those claimants to al-qadar thereby. He legislated for them to utilize arks by His commandment, ordering them and their followers to sail upon them within the ocean of fate. He exempted those who sailed in them for salvation just as He exempted the people of the Ark and made it a clear sign for the creation. The adherents of the commandments are a war for the *Qadariyyah,*[69] persisting in that until they revert them back to the commandments. Likewise, the *Qadariyyah* wage war against the people of the commandments, doing so until they ultimately take them away from it. The religion of the Messengers (عَلَيْهِمُ السَّلَامُ) is (compliance with) commandments while believing in predestiny and arbitrating (fate) with (revealed) commandment. Iblīs and his acolytes have (made) fate and rejection of (revealed) commandment as their religion. So reflect over this issue of predestiny and (revealed) commandment, and how the world split into these groups.[70]

The Innateness of Believing in Allah's Providence

Even before the advent of Islam, the Arabs had remained upon an innate belief about Allah's authority over the universe,

[68] Maryam: 83

[69] meaning all of the sects that deviate pertaining the belief in al qadar.

[70] Rawḍah al Muḥibbīn pp. 61-63. Dar al Kutub al 'Ilmiyyah 1403/1983

contrary to the many civilizations surrounding them in all directions. Al Imām Abūl Qāsim Hibatullah al-Lālakā'ī (رَحِمَهُ ٱللَّهُ) (died 418 h.) said:

> Ahmad b. Yahyā Tha'lab[71] (رَحِمَهُ ٱللَّهُ) said: I do not know of an Arab who is a Qadarī (i.e. a denier of predestination). It was said to him: Does the statement (denying) predestination even occur to the hearts of the Arabs? He responded: Allah's refuge is sought! There are none amongst the Arabs except that they affirm the predestination of both the good and the bad, **this was the case with the people both during *Jāhiliyyah*[72] and Islam**. That is found replete throughout their poetry and their speech.
>
> Al Hāfiz Abul Qāsim (Al-Lālakā'ī) (رَحِمَهُ ٱللَّهُ) said: Without doubt, it is the way of Ahl Al-Sunnah, inherited generation after generation since the time of Allah's Messenger, and all praise is due to Allah for that; and I ask Allah, by His bounty and mercy, for its entirety.[73]

Tha'lab (رَحِمَهُ ٱللَّهُ) is an uncontested authority on the Arabic language, which is, of course, an essential facet of Arab and Islamic culture. Therefore, he was deeply knowledgeable about the poetry and traditions of the Arabs dating back for ages, and as such was qualified to make such an assertion. The above statement of Tha'lab is quite revealing in highlighting the fact that even during the era of pre-Islamic ignorance, the Arabs believed in divine predestination and preordainment of everything that happens. This was a tradition that very likely traces all the way back to Abraham and Ishmael (عَلَيْهِمَا ٱلسَّلَامُ) in antiquity. This is an important point to highlight the nature of

71 He is commonly known simply as Tha'lab — one of three scholars constituting the foundation of the famous Kufic school of grammar during his era and thereafter. He is a renowned scholar of language and ḥadīth, Abūl 'Abbās Aḥmad b. Yaḥyā b. Zayd b. Sayār al Baghdādī al-Shaybānī; the author of Al Faṣīh and Al-Taṣānīf. He was born in the year 200 h. in Baghdād during the reign of Ma'mūn and died in Baghdād in the year 291 h.

72 i.e. pre-Islamic barbarism

73 Al-Lālakā'ī. Sharḥ Usūl 'Itiqād Ahl al-Sunnah; Article 941 vol. 3, p. 593

their polytheism being primarily by way of appointing intercessors between Man and Creator, as opposed to directly assigning Divine Attributes to their idols.

Belief in Qadar is the Connecting Thread of Monotheism

Based on what has preceded, the belief in predestiny is inseparable from monotheism, as 'Abd Allah b. 'Abbās (رَضِيَٱللَّهُعَنْهُمَا) stated:

> الْقَدَرُ نِظَامُ التَّوْحِيدِ, فَمَنْ وَحَّدَ اللَّهَ عَزَّ وَجَلَّ, وَآمَنَ بِالْقَدَرِ, فَهِيَ الْعُرْوَةُ الْوُثْقَى الَّتِي لَا انْفِصَامَ لَهَا, وَمَنْ وَحَّدَ اللَّهَ تَعَالَى, وَكَذَّبَ بِالْقَدَرِ, نَقْضَ التَّوْحِيدَ
>
> Predestination is the connecting thread of monotheism. So whoever singles out Allah عَزَّوَجَلَّ (as the sole deity) and believes in the Qadar, then that is the strongest handhold, unable to be broken. Whereas, whoever singles out Allah (تَبَارَكَوَتَعَالَىٰ) (as the sole deity) while belying the Qadar, invalidates monotheism.[74]

Ibn Abī-l 'Izz al Ḥanafī (رَحِمَهُٱللَّهُ) explains:

> And that is because belief in *al-qadar* includes **belief in Allah's eternal knowledge**, and what He had shown of His knowledge cannot be encompassed. Also (it includes) all that He has written of the creation's destinies. Many people have strayed in this instance, including the polytheists, the *Ṣabians*,[75] and the philosophers — the latter reject Allah's knowledge of detailed components or other than that. All of that is considered as belying *al qadar*. As for **Allah's power** over all things, then that is what the *Qadariyyah* broadly reject, in as

74 *Ḥasan li Ghayrihi.* Reported by 'Abdullah b. Aḥmad b. Ḥanbal in Al-Sunnah, articles 925 & 928; Al Faryābī in Al Qadar article 205; Al Ajūrī in Al-Sharī'ah p. 197; Ibn Baṭṭah al 'Ukbarī in Al Ibānah al Kubrā, articles 1618-1619; Al-Lālakā'ī in Sharḥ Usūl 'Itiqād Ahl Al-Sunnah, articles 1112 & 1224.

75 the Ṣabians are discussed in the next chapter and other subsequent chapters.

much as that they deem Him to not have created the actions of the slaves. So they excluded that from being by Allah's power and creation.[76]

Likewise, Al Imām Aḥmad (رَحِمَهُ ٱللَّهُ) famously said, when asked about *al Qadar*:

القَدَرُ قُدْرَةُ اللهِ

"Al Qadar is Allah's power."[77]

Ibn al Qayyim (رَحِمَهُ ٱللَّهُ) comments on this statement saying:

> Ibn 'Aqīl (رَحِمَهُ ٱللَّهُ) greatly approved of this statement and said: "This shows the intricate knowledge of Aḥmad (رَحِمَهُ ٱللَّهُ) and his depth in knowing the foundations of the religion." The matter is just as Abul Wafā' (رَحِمَهُ ٱللَّهُ) stated. For certainly, denying al Qadar is a denial of the power of Al-Rabb (the Nurturing Lord) over creating, writing and preordaining His creations actions.[78]

Likewise, the great scholar 'Abd al-Rahmān b. Nāṣir al-Sa'dī (رَحِمَهُ ٱللَّهُ) said:

> Included within unity of Lordship (*tawḥīd al-rubūbiyyah*) is affirming divine predestination and preordainment, that whatever Allah (تَبَارَكَ وَتَعَالَىٰ) wills comes to pass, while whatever He does not will would not happen, and that he He is *Al Ghaniyy, Al Ḥamīd* (Free of need. Worthy of All Praise).[79]

Likewise, Ibn al Qayyim (رَحِمَهُ ٱللَّهُ) explains in many places in his writings why belief in predestination is the connecting thread of monotheism. He says:

---

76 Ibn b. Abī-l 'Izz al Ḥanafī. Sharḥ al 'Aqīdah al-Ṭahāwiyyah, p. 249..

77 Ibn Taymiyyah. Majmū' al Fatāwā 8/308; Ṭarīq al Hijratayn p. 170; Shafā' al 'Alīl p. 59.

78 Ibn Qayyim al Jawziyyah. Shifā' al 'Alīl p. 59-60.

79 Al-Sa'dī. Al Mukhtaṣar fī Usūl al 'Aqā'id al-Dīniyyah

> In summary: every evidence for monotheism in the *Qurān* is simultaneously an evidence for predestination and that the servants' actions are created. As such, affirmation of predestination is the foundation of monotheism, as Ibn 'Abbās (رَضِيَ اللَّهُ عَنْهُمَا) said.[80]

Elsewhere, Ibn al Qayyim رَحِمَهُ اللَّهُ explains further:

> Belief in predestination is the foundation of belief in divine command (i.e. the revelation), and it is the connecting thread of monotheism. So whoever belies predestination, then his denial has invalidated his faith.[81]

In *Shifā' al 'Alīl*, his detailed book about the belief in al Qadar, he explains even further:

> Prior preordainment aids in doing deeds, it drives one thereto and it necessitates their occurrence. It does not contradict or obstruct one from (the concept of) doing them. This is a place where a foot slips. Whoever's footing is firm upon it, then he succeeds in achieving abiding bliss, whereas whoever's foot slipped, plunges into the pit of hellfire. So, as regards *al-qadar*, the Prophet (صَلَّى اللَّهُ عَلَيْهِ وَسَلَّمَ) instructed his nation pertaining two matters that are the dual cause of felicity: (1) believing in preordainment, for indeed that is the connecting threat of monotheism; while (2) attending to the causal means that lead to the good of (what is preordained) and restrain against the bad of it, for indeed that is the connecting thread of the revealed law. Therefore, he (صَلَّى اللَّهُ عَلَيْهِ وَسَلَّمَ) directed them to the connecting thread of both monotheism and the (divine) commandment. Yet the deviants refused except to berate by means of either denial of the root of monotheism or by way of affirmation of the root of revealed law. Their minds — which Allah (تَبَارَكَ وَتَعَالَى) had not cast light into — could not accommodate harmonizing

80 Ibn Qayyim al Jawziyyah. Shifā' al 'Alīl p. 65

81 Rawḍah al Muḥibbīn p. 61

between what the Prophets all reconciled between, namely, divine predestiny and revealed law: both Creating and Commanding.

﴿فَهَدَى اللَّهُ الَّذِينَ آمَنُوا لِمَا اخْتَلَفُوا فِيهِ مِنَ الْحَقِّ بِإِذْنِهِ وَاللَّهُ يَهْدِي مَن يَشَاءُ إِلَىٰ صِرَاطٍ مُّسْتَقِيمٍ﴾

"Then Allah by His Leave guided those who believed to the truth of that wherein they differed. And Allah guides whom He wills to a Straight Path."[82]

The Prophet (صَلَّى ٱللَّٰهُ عَلَيْهِ وَسَلَّمَ) was extremely adamant in harmonizing these two matters for his nation...He said:

احْرِصْ عَلَى مَا يَنْفَعُكَ، وَاسْتَعِنْ بِاللهِ وَلَا تَعْجَزْ

Be diligent upon what benefits you, seek Allah's help and do not be lazy." The lazy person is the one who cannot accommodate both matters.[83]

Al-Shaykh al-Sa'dī (رَحِمَهُ ٱللَّٰهُ) (died 1356 h.) explains how the entire religion is contained within the concept of complying with divine commandments while simultaneously trusting in Allah's inerrant control of all things. He explains that the entire religion is built upon the verse in the Fātiḥah:

﴿إِيَّاكَ نَعْبُدُ وَإِيَّاكَ نَسْتَعِينُ﴾

"You alone do we worship, and your aid alone do we seek."

He further elaborates:

By the servant's completion of worshipping Allah while seeking His assistance, then his religious and worldly affairs will be perfected. So worshipping Allah entails that the servant undertakes singling Allah out (as the sole deity), worshipping Him outwardly, inwardly, monetarily and bodily, and with a combination of both. It is also related to both Allah's rights and

[82] Al Baqarah: 213.

[83] Ibn Qayyim al Jawziyyah. Shifā' al 'Alīl, p. 121.

the rights of the creation. That includes establishment of all that is of a comprehensive and beneficial interest for the Muslims pertaining their religiosity as well as their worldly life.

This undertaking is to be accompanied by three matters:

(1) Strong effort and diligence in accordance with the worshipper's capacity.
(2) Strong reliance upon Allah in easing that matter being attempted by the servant, while having full confidence that Allah will ease it.
(3) Complete sincerity for Allah, whereas the motive for his implementation should not be for some lowly ambition or to be seen and heard by people. Nor should it be out of fanaticism, nationalism, or racial pride. Instead, the motivation to do that should be intending Allah's good-pleasure and to procure His reward. The beneficial advantages stemming off from that are a part of His Reward.

Upon adopting this comprehensive concept, it becomes clear to us that undertaking all of the advantageous available means as well as whatever completes and complements them is from the greatest of meanings included in this maxim.[84]

Also, in his commentary on the *Sunan* of Abū Dawūd, Ibn al Qayyim رَحِمَهُ ٱللَّهُ says:

> That which is alluded to by the statement of Ibn Mas'ūd رَضِيَ ٱللَّهُ عَنْهُ is what all of the Ṣaḥābah رَضِيَ ٱللَّهُ عَنْهُمْ and the Imāms of Sunnah from the Tabi'īn and those after them رَحِمَهُمُ ٱللَّهُ abided by. It is the affirmation of predestiny, which is the connecting thread of monotheism, whilst simultaneously affirming chosen behavior for the servants, which is the connected thread of (divine) commandment and prohibition. Even further, this also pertains

84 Usūl 'Aẓīmah min Qawā'id al Islām, p. 15-16. Maktabah Dar al Minhāj (1432).

to divine commendation and contempt, as well as divine reward and punishment.[85]

So to summarize: the first matter is that of **predestination** through Allah's Omniscience, Omnipotence, Wisdom, and Lordship. The second matter is that of **divine revelation** and commandment which is met by the person with either compliance or noncompliance according to their exercise of personal will and ability — which were likewise created and predestined by the Creator. The third matter is that of **divine praise and dispraise**, and reward and punishment, which is the causal result of the combination of the first two things, and, likewise, occurs by way of divine predestination and preordainment.

So no people have ever strayed throughout history except because of misunderstanding or doubting the extent of Allah's sovereignty and Providence over the creation. Shaykh al Islām Ibn Taymiyyah رَحِمَهُ ٱللَّهُ famously stated in his poem about the belief in Qadar, that is known as *al-Ta'iyyah*, in refutation of a Christian sceptic of predestiny:

وأَصْلُ ضَلاَلِ الخَلْقِ مِنْ كُلِّ فِرْقَةٍ ** هُوَ الخَوْضُ فِي فِعْلِ الإِلَهِ بِعِلَّةٍ

The root of the deviation of every sect is delving into the reasons for Allah's actions.

فَإِنَّهُمو لَمْ يَفْهَمُوا حِكْمَةً لَهُ ** فَصَارُوا عَلَى نَوْعٍ مِنَ الجَاهِلِيَّةِ

They did not understand the Wisdom that He has and as such they became in a type of *Jāhiliyyah*.

فإِنَّ جَمِيعَ الكَوْنِ أَوْجَبَ فِعْلَهُ ** مَشِيئَةُ ربِّ الخَلْقِ بَارِى الخَلِيقة

What necessitated the doing of the entire universe was nothing but the Will of the creation's Lord and Maker.

وذَاتُ إِلَهِ الخَلْقِ وَاجِبَةٌ بِمَا ** لَهَا مِنْ صِفَاتٍ واجباتٍ قَدِيمَةٍ

85 Hāshiyah Ibn al Qayyim 'alā Tahdhīb al-Sunan, vol. 6, p. 105.

The Dhāt (i.e., essence and existence) of the creation's God is a necessity along with what it necessarily has of Eternal Attributes:

مَشِيئَتُه مَعَ عِلْمِهِ ثُمَّ قُدْرَةٍ ** لَوَازِمُ ذاتِ اللهِ قَاضي القَضِيَّةِ

His (Divine) **Will** along with His **Knowledge** and then (His) **Power** are inseparable from Allah's essence, who is the Arbiter in (this and every) matter.

وَإِبْدَاعُه مَا شَاءَ مِنْ مُبْدَعَاتِهِ ** بِهَا حِكْمَةٌ فِيهِ وأَنْوَاعُ رَحْمَةِ

His **originating** what He wills from His works is by way of **Wisdom** entailed therein and assortments of **Mercy.**

In summary, the orthodox Muslim belief about predestiny and fate is an essential extension of our fundamental belief in: His Existence; His Omniscience; His Will and Choice; His Omnipotence and being the Sole Creator; His Wisdom; and His Mercy. This is a crucial belief that must be had in order to protect a person from pessimism and despair. Without understanding it a person cannot adequately cope with the trials of life and will very likely pit reason against revelation and doubt the Providence of our Merciful Creator, as has occurred since the earliest times.

In his book *al Fawā'id*, Ibn al Qayyim رَحِمَهُ ٱللَّهُ provides some useful outlooks directly related to sound belief in Allah's Perfect Attributes that comfort people during hardships. He says:

> Whenever something predestined happens to a person that he dislikes, then there are six outlooks for him pertaining it:
>
> *The First* is the perspective of *al-tawḥīd* (Allah's Oneness): that it was Allah (تَبَارَكَ وَتَعَالَىٰ) that predestined, preordained, and created it; whatever Allah (تَبَارَكَ وَتَعَالَىٰ) wills happens and whatever He does not will does not happen.
>
> *The Second* the perspective of *al 'Adl* (Justice): Allah's judgment regarding Him has been executed and His ordainment if fair.

The Third is the perspective of *al-Raḥmah* (Mercy): that Allah's Mercy is more abundant than His Anger and Retribution, and His Mercy surrounds him.

The Fourth is the perspective of *al Ḥikmah* (Wisdom): that His Wisdom necessitated that; He did not predestine it without purpose, nor did He preordain it in jest.

The Fifth is the perspective of *al Ḥamd* (Praiseworthiness): that Allah deserves praise for that in every way.

The Sixth is the perspective of al *'ubūdiyyah* (servitude): that one is nothing more than a servant in every way. The laws and ordainments of his Master apply to him by merit of his being His property and servant. He manages him under His judgments of predestiny just as He manages him under His religious laws. He is the recipient of these laws which are applicable to him.[86]

Conclusion: Destructive Thoughts about the Creator

Ibn al Qayyim (رَحِمَهُ ٱللَّهُ) said, "Indeed, the greatest of sins in Allah's estimation is harboring bad thoughts about Him. For certainly, the one who thinks poorly about Him has thought about Him that which opposes His Holy Perfection."[87] What immediately preceded in this chapter shows us that a hopeless, dark, pessimistic ontology and worldview can only result from a lack of correctly understanding the perfection of the Creator's Knowledge, Will, Power, Wisdom, and Mercy. It likewise results from a failure of imagination pertaining how to achieve the most favorable outcomes in our lives by compliance with His commandments. In short, such a person doubts the extent of Divine Providence and Allah's involvement in the world and does not see compliance with divine commandments as a solution to humanity's problems and crises. The pessimistic, hopeless, and

[86] Ibn Qayyim al Jawziyyah. Al Fawā'id p. 32.

[87] Al Jawāb al Kāfī p. 138.

directionless outlooks of such people are a direct result of not knowing the Greatness and Goodness of their Creator.

Ibn al Qayyim (رَحِمَهُ ٱللَّهُ) further elaborates on the state of humanity when reacting to the hardships of life in *Zād al Ma'ād*, saying:

> Most people think about Allah what is not true, thinking wrongly about (Him) pertaining what is particular to themselves and about what He does to others. None are safe from that except for those who know Allah, know His Names and Attributes, and know what His Praiseworthiness and Wisdom necessitate. Whoever loses hope in His Mercy or despairs of His Help has thought wrongly about Him...
>
> In summary, whoever thinks about Him contrary to what He described Himself with and what His Messengers عَلَيْهِمُ ٱلسَّلَامُ described him with, or negates the literal meanings of what He described Himself with and what His Messengers described Him with, has thought wrong thoughts about Him...
>
> So most of the Creation, or rather, all of them — except those whom Allah spares — think what is untrue about Allah, harboring evil thoughts. Most of the sons of Adam believe that they are cheated from what they deserve and have less than their fair share — that they deserve above and beyond what Allah (تَبَارَكَ وَتَعَالَىٰ) has given them. Their actions say: My Lord has oppressed me and deprived me from what I deserve. His own self (inwardly) testifies to that while his tongue denies it and does not have the audacity to declare it. Whoever investigates his own self and deeply plunges into awareness of its hidden facets will see this latent within him, like fire being applied to a fuse. Lite the fuse of whoever you choose and his sparks will tell you about his fuse. Were you to examine anyone, you would find some level of intolerance for what is predestined: that they blame it, suggest that it should have been contrary to what

happened, and that it should have been such and such. Some do this to a little and some do this a lot.[88]

As is discussed in these two volumes and has been alluded to in this chapter, the core of revealed religion is belief and compliance, whereas the core of all deviance is pitting reason against faith because of discounting Divine Providence. This conflicted state is representative of the creeds of the ancient pagans and it remains until today as the ethos of modernity. It is the common thread that gathers the deviant sects of philosophers and mystics alongside those who share a similar outlook at the world. It is the foundation of the ideological assault and its underlying strategy. Understanding it provides us with a basis for understanding the rise and fall of nations in general, and the decline of Muslim civilization in particular.

---

[88] See Zād al Ma'ād, p. 205-208.

Part II: the Foundations of Western Culture

The Three Interconnected Foundations of all Misguidance

Before proceeding further, it is imperative to highlight the three interconnected foundations of deviation.[89] The first is having a pessimistic outlook and negative thoughts about the Creator. The second is doubting the Creator's Wisdom and Authority over this world. The third is pitting human reason against revealed religion. These three things are inseparable and constitute the foundation of all deviation; and where we find one, then the others are nearby. They mutual reinforce and reproduce each other, and have done so all throughout human history. They blend and merge with each other, making it difficult for even the most trained eye to identify where one begins, and another ends. If instead of noting the differences, we looked at the similarities and commonalities between ancient pagan belief systems, then we would see these foundations squarely at their core. In summary, evil thoughts about the Creator result in discounting the Creator's Wise Rulership over the world, which, in turn, results in pitting human reason against revealed religion. Despite the infinite complexities and complication of polytheistic doctrines, this is the most useful starting point to unravel their mysteries and expose their toxic core. Some details of this have preceded in the previous chapter, but are worth reiterating at this point.

At the conclusion of the previous chapter we outlined how the source of all deviation stems from hopelessness and having bad thoughts about the Creator. Recall the statement of Ibn al Qayyim رَحِمَهُ ٱللَّهُ who said, "Indeed, the greatest of sins in Allah's

---

[89] discussed in Chapter 2 of Islamophobia and the Ideological Assault Vol. 1.

estimation is harboring bad thoughts about Him. For certainly, the one who thinks poorly about Him has thought about Him that which opposes His Holy Perfection."[90] Also, recall his statement, "Most people think about Allah what is not true, thinking wrongly about (Him) pertaining what is particular to themselves and what He does to others. None are safe from doing so except for those who know Allah, know His Names and Attributes, and know what His Praiseworthiness and Wisdom necessitate. Whoever loses hope in His Mercy or despairs of His Help has thought wrongly about Him"[91] The current chapter traces the origins of this pessimistic outlook and its outcomes from antiquity and how that has shaped Western thought ever since. The hopeless outlook leads directly to the second strand of misguidance which is discounting Divine Providence and questioning Allah's Authority over the world. Recall the statement of Ibn Taymiyyah رَحِمَهُ ٱللَّهُ in his poem about predestiny, "The root of the deviation of every sect is delving into the reasons for Allah's actions."

Recall from the previous chapter how al-Lālakā'ī رَحِمَهُ ٱللَّهُ explained at length that this questioning of Allah's Wisdom and Authority is what led people to pitting human reason against divine revelation.[92] This is the third foundation of misguidance. Ibn al Qayyim says in al-Ṣawā'iq al Mursala, "(Iblīs) was the first to counter revelation with mortal reason, granting primacy to the intellect...**This chieftain passed on this conflict as a legacy to his students. Ever since, every trial and tribulation for the Prophets and their followers has emanated therefrom."** Here, Ibn al Qayyim has provided us with an invaluable lens to view all of history from. He says, "The basis of

[90] Ibn al Qayyim. Al Jawāb al Kāfi, p. 138.

[91] Ibn al Qayyim. Zād al Ma'ād, p. 205.

[92] See pp. 48-50.

of every calamity in the universe, is as Muḥammad al-Shahrastānī stated: from pitting human reason against divine revelation and granting precedence to whimsicalities over the religion. The people are engulfed in the evils of this conflict until the present day."[93]

The three-pronged devastation caused by pessimism, discounting Divine Providence, and pitting human reason against revealed religion has a final outcome and end result which is (1) negation of the Creator's Divine Attributes (ta'ṭīl) and (2) polytheism (shirk). This chapter discusses the worldwide spread of ta'ṭīl and shirk that was constructed upon the aforementioned foundations of misguidance.

Syncretism

Negative theology (*al-ṭa'ṭīl*) and polytheism (*al-shirk*) took various forms throughout history and those varying forms eventually merged and blended with each other as time progressed. This process is referred to as **syncretism** which is commonly defined as "the combination or attempted blending of different religions, cultures, or schools of thought." The historical process of syncretism extends from antiquity, since the time of the Prophet Abraham (عَلَيْهِ الصَّلَاةُ وَالسَّلَامُ) and the *Ṣabians* of Harran. The above definition of syncretism perfectly matches Ibn al Qayyim's description of the *Ṣabians,* whose approach constituted the cornerstone of Greek philosophy and has continued on uninterrupted ever since:

> The core of their affair is that they claim to take the appealing aspects found with the adherents of different religions, not having allegiance or disavowal for one religion or another nor

[93] Ibn al Qayyim. Mukhtaṣar al-Ṣawā'iq, vol. 1, p. 178.

> having fanaticism for any religion over another. In their view, the religions are spiritual matters necessary for the greater good of the world.

Meaning that although they did not believe in these religions, they saw that religion in general has a pragmatic utility that is necessary for social stability and order, and so they hand-picked and piece-mailed a civic religion together from different religions.

This ancient syncretic mentality remains the default approach of Western thought until today. The political scientist and social historian Carrol Quigley states, "the social unfolding of the truth, is the basis of the Western religious outlook. This outlook believed that religious truth unfolded in time and is not yet complete."[94] He elaborates elsewhere:

> Western religious thought has continued to believe that **revelation itself is never final, total, complete, or literal, but is a continuous symbolic process that must be interpreted and reinterpreted by discussion**. The method of the West, even in religion, has been this: The truth unfolds in time by a cooperative process of discussion that creates a temporary consensus which we hope will form successive approximations growing closer and closer to the final truth, to be reached only in some final stage of eternity.[95]

As this first volume outlines, the reinterpretation of revealed religion by ideas rooted in mysticism and philosophy is the reality of this "social unfolding of the truth" that is the basis of the Western religious outlook that believed that "religious truth unfolded in time and is not yet complete." This attitude is

---

94 Quigley. The Evolution of Civilizations, pp. 341-342.

95 Quigley. Tragedy and Hope, pp. 1229-1231.

credited as being the cause of Western progress. Quigley explains the Western model:

> It has six parts: 1. There is a truth, a reality. 2. No person, group, or organization has the whole picture of the truth. (Thus there is no absolute or final authority.) 3. Every person of goodwill has some aspect of the truth, some vision of it from the angle of his own experience. (Thus each has something to contribute.) 4. Through discussion, the aspects of the truth held by many can be pooled and arranged to form a consensus closer to the truth than any of the sources that contributed to it. 5. This consensus is a temporary approximation of the truth, which is no sooner made than new experiences and additional information make it possible for it to be reformulated in a closer approximation of the truth by continued discussion. 6. **Thus Western man's picture of the truth advances, by successive approximations, closer and closer to the whole truth without ever reaching it. This methodology of the West is basic to the success, power, and wealth of Western Civilization. It is reflected in all successful aspects of Western life, from the earliest beginnings to the present.**

The aforementioned common tendency towards syncretism in Western thought was exploited long ago to hijack and change both the meanings and the record of the revelation given to the Prophets (عَلَيۡهِمُ السَّلَامُ). Obvious signs of syncretic borrowing from pagan sources exist in Judaism, Christianity, and even in some aberrational interpretations of Islam. The authors of both the Jewish and Christian scriptures are obscure and mostly unknown. The scribes who later recorded the earlier oral tradition claimed to have been under divine inspiration when writing. It is notable that their communities were immersed within and subjugated by pagan cultures when these writings were produced. The earliest written copies of the Torah date back to the time of Jewish captivity in Babylon and show unmistakable signs of syncretic influence. The same can be said about much of the Old Testament and of Jewish theology.

The conquests of Alexander two centuries later would put Jewish theology on a trajectory of being directly impacted by Greek philosophy, which itself was a syncretic blend of Greek, Persian, and Egyptian thought, as is explained later in this chapter. The same holds true of the earliest Christian scriptures and theology, as is likewise discussed near the end of this chapter. Some of the most robust implications of how syncretism altered the Jewish and Christian interpretations of revealed religion point towards Zoroastrianism, the ancient religion of the Magus of Persia. Just as this view holds strong merit when looking at its impact on the Jews, on the Greek philosophers, and subsequently on the Christians, then it also carries significant weight when applied to the pessimistic esoteric doctrines of Persian and Greek origin that infiltrated Muslim civilization in its early days, precipitating its eventual decline.

After first discussing the connection of polytheism and ta'ṭīl with bad thoughts about Allah and a pessimistic ontology, this chapter outlines the origins and final product of Greek philosophy — tracing it from its ancient roots of paganism, magic, and mysticism to its ultimate deification of Man and human reason rooted in the very same mysticism and magic. This sets the stage for the paganization of Christianity and, after that, the crisis of Islam through the onslaught of similar doctrines.

The Ancient Regime: Polytheism & Negativist Theology

Al Shirk wal-Ta'ṭīl (polytheism & negating Allah's Attributes) form the greatest foundation of mankind's hopelessness throughout the ages. In *Ighātha al-Lahfān,* Ibn al Qayyim رَحِمَهُ ٱللَّٰهُ explains that polytheism and negating Allah's Attributes are connected to each other and that both emanate from thinking poorly about Allah. He says:

> Polytheism and ta'ṭīl (negating Allah's attributes) are built upon having bad thoughts about Allah.
>
> ﴿أَإِفْكًا آلِهَةً دُونَ اللَّهِ تُرِيدُونَ فَمَا ظَنُّكُم بِرَبِّ الْعَالَمِينَ﴾
>
> "[86.] 'Is it a falsehood — other deities beside Allah that you seek? [87.] Then what do you think about the Lord of the 'Alamin (mankind, jinns, and all that exists)?'"[96]

Although the meaning is: What do think about how He will deal with you and recompense you, while you had worshipped others and assigned rivals to Him? Then you will find under this threat: What bad thoughts did you have about your Lord to such an extent that you worshiped others alongside Him?

The polytheist thinks that Allah (تَبَارَكَ وَتَعَالَى) needs other entities to administer the affairs of the world along with Him, such as a minister, supporter or helper. This is the worst denigration of One who, in His essence, is Free of Need from everything besides Himself, while everything besides Him, in its nature, is direly in need of Him. Or he thinks that Allah's power is only complete through that of a counterpart. Or (he thinks) that He does not know until an intermediary informs Him, or will not show mercy until an intermediary persuades Him to be merciful, or that He alone is not sufficient for His servants. Or (he thinks) that He will not do what His servant wants until an intermediary intercedes on his behalf — as people vouch for each other. So (he thinks) his intervention needs to be accepted because He needs and benefits from an intercessor, as though He strengthens and honors Himself by doing so. Or (he thinks) that He will not answer His servant's summonings until they ask an intermediary to present their needs to Him, as is the condition of the kings of the world.

[96] Al-Ṣāfāt: 86-87.

This is the root of the polytheism of the creation. Or he thinks that He does not hear their supplications until intermediaries first present them because He is far from them. Or he feels that a particular created being has some right upon Him, so he swears by that thing because of its right upon Him, using that thing as a means (for His answering a supplication), just as people held in high esteem or who are unopposable employ each to reach nobles or kings.

All of this is a denigration of (Allah's) Lordship and a detraction from its rights. The diminishment in the polytheist's heart of love, fear, hope, reliance, and turning to Him is terrible enough. This is because they divide that in shares between Him and those assigned as His counterparts — causing their reverence, love, fear, and hope to diminish or disappear, having redirected it in full or in part to those that they worshipped besides Him. **Polytheism necessitates denigration of Al-Rabb** (the Nurturing Lord and Creator). Belittlement is necessarily its prerequisite, whether or not the polytheists do so out of volition or refuse to concede that this is the case. As such, His Praiseworthiness and Perfect Lordship necessitate that He does not forgive it and that He places its practitioner eternally in painful torment. He has judged him to be the most miserable of creatures.

So you will never find a polytheist except that they denigrate Allah, even if they claim that they are honoring Him thereby. Likewise, you will not find an innovator except that He denigrates the Prophet, although he insists that he is respecting the Prophet ﷺ through his innovation. This is so because he claims that this is better than the Sunnah and closer to correctness, or may even assert that it is the Sunnah. If he has clear sight about what his innovation is, then he is an opponent of Allah and the Messenger. Thus, those who are degrading and degraded with Allah, His Messenger, and His allies are the adherents to polytheism and innovation.[97]

The Two Strands of Polytheism

Both Ibn Taymiyyah and Ibn al Qayyim (رَحِمَهُمَا ٱللَّهُ) repeatedly explain the connections between the strands of polytheism present in the ancient world with those in the Muslim world during their time. They connect the syncretic *Ṣabian* tradition, dating back in antiquity to the time and people of the patriarch Prophet Abraham (عَلَيْهِ ٱلصَّلَاةُ وَٱلسَّلَامُ), to the negation of Divine Attributes and the mystical occult practices of some of the philosophers in the Muslim world shortly before their time. Ibn Taymiyyah (رَحِمَهُ ٱللَّهُ) says in *al-Radd ʿalā-l Manṭiqiyyīn*:

> The vast majority of polytheism within humanity emanates from two origins: The first is **revering the graves of the righteous and replicating their images in an attempt to seek blessing**. This is the first means by which humanity innovated polytheism, accounting for the polytheism of Noah's people. Ibn ʿAbbās (رَضِيَ ٱللَّهُ عَنْهُمَا) said, "There were ten generations between Adam and Noah (عَلَيْهِمَا ٱلسَّلَامُ), all of which practiced monotheism." It is also established in the Ṣaḥīḥ from the Prophet (صَلَّى ٱللَّهُ عَلَيْهِ وَسَلَّمَ) that he said, "Verily Noah (عَلَيْهِ ٱلسَّلَامُ) was the first Messenger dispatched to the people of Earth." Accordingly, Allah (عَزَّ وَجَلَّ) did not mention there being any messenger prior to him, in as much that polytheism surfaced during his time...
>
> **The second cause (of polytheism) is the worshipping of the cosmos.** They used to make talismans devoted to the cosmos, carefully observing the special occasion to make each

[97] Ibn Qayyim al Jawziyyah. Ighātha al-Lahfān p. 62-64.

talisman. They would construct it from a substance[98] that they believed to have a connection suited to the nature of that planet and utter polytheistic statements of disbelief upon it, at which point demons would converse with them and fulfill their needs. They would call them cosmic spirits, whereas, in truth, it was merely a male or female demon misleading them. As for the book that someone wrote called *Al-Sirr al Maktūm fī al Siḥr wa Mukhbāṭabah al-Nujūm* (the hidden secret of magic and conversing with the stars—authored by Fakhr al-Dīn al-Rāzī), then that without doubt traces back to the polytheism of the Chaldean Kashdāns that Al Khalīl (i.e. Abraham عَلَيْهِ السَّلَامُ) was sent to, and it is from the highest degrees of sorcery. Accordingly, the Prophet (صَلَّى ٱللَّهُ عَلَيْهِ وَسَلَّمَ) said in the ḥadīth collect by Abū Dawūd and others:

مَنْ اقْتَبَسَ شُعْبَةً مِن النُّجُومِ فَقَد اقْتَبَسَ شُعْبَةً مِن السِّحْرِ زَادَ مَا زَادَ

"Whoever acquires a portion of astrology has acquired a portion of sorcery, and it (i.e. sorcery) increases the more he increases (in learning astrology)."

...For indeed Ḥarrān was the abode of these *Ṣabians*, and Ibrahim (عَلَيْهِ السَّلَامُ) was either born there or he later moved there from Iraq according to the two different views. It contained the Temple of the First Mind, the temple of the Self, the temple of Saturn, the temple of Jupiter, the temple of Mars, the temple of the Sun, and likewise those devoted to Venus, Mercury, and the Moon.[99]

Elsewhere, Ibn Taymiyyah (رَحِمَهُ ٱللَّهُ) elaborates more on the connection between the occultist philosophers of the Muslim world and the syncretism of the ancient Ṣabians existent ever since the time of Ibrahīm:

---

[98] such as a precious or semi-precious stone or metal.

[99] Al-Radd 'alā al Manṭiqiyyīn, p. 287. Dār al Ma'rifah, Beirut.

> There are some that ascribe to Islām who have written books about the way of the polytheistic Ṣabians in worshipping celestial bodies, claiming thereby that they were attempting to use that as a medium for worldly objectives, including monarchical rule and other such matters. These writings are from the sorcery of the Canaanites whose kings were titled Namāridah (sing. Nimrod) — to whom Allah sent His Khalīl (i.e. beloved) Abraham (عَلَيْهِ ٱلسَّلَامُ) with the religion of monotheism and sincere worship.[100]

Due to their worship of the cosmos, historians call the peoples of that ancient era the cosmological civilizations. Ibn al Qayyim (رَحِمَهُ ٱللَّهُ) further explains the *Ṣabian* precedent for contemporary deviations. He says in *Miftāḥ Dār al-Sa'ādah*:

> Did Ibrahim (عَلَيْهِ ٱلسَّلَامُ) ever have another enemy comparable to these Ṣabian astrologers? Ḥarrān was the abode of their kingdom, and al Khalīl (i.e. Ibrahim) (عَلَيْهِ ٱلسَّلَامُ) was their worst enemy. They are the true polytheist, and the idols that they used to worship were images and statues representing celestial bodies. They used to devote temples — which are houses of worship— to them. Each celestial body had its temple containing the idols associated with it. So their worship and adoration of idols were, in fact, reverence and worship for the heavenly bodies that they made these idols to commemorate. This is the stronger of the two causes of the polytheism that transpires in the world, namely, associationism and veneration related to the stars: believing them to be living, speaking entities, possessing spirits that descend upon their worshippers and those who converse with them. So they fashioned earthly images of them and made their worship and reverence the means to worship these celestial bodies and to summon their spirits. Thereupon, the devils descend upon them, to dialogue and converse with them, showing them wondrous things that enticed them to sacrifice their lives, children, and wealth for the

---

[100] Iqtiḍā' al-Ṣirāṭ al Mustaqīm, p. 219. Dar 'Aalam al Kutub, Beirut. (1419/1999).

sake of these idols and to draw nearer to them. The starting point of this polytheism was venerating the celestial bodies and believing that fortune and misfortune and the occurrence of good and evil in the world came from them. **This is the polytheism of the elite associationists and their speculative theologians**. It was the polytheism of Ibrahim's people.

The second cause is the worship of graves and making the dead into counterparts with the Divine, which was the polytheism of Noah's people: it was the first polytheism to penetrate the world. Its temptation is broader and those afflicted with it are greater in number. They consist of the masses of the practitioners of polytheism. Often this will apply to a particular polytheist — that he is both a grave-worshipper and star-worshipper... The former (i.e., worshippers of the graves of saints) were the enemies of Noah (عَلَيْهِ ٱلسَّلَامُ), just as those who deemed the stars to be divine counterparts were the enemies of Abraham. The hostility of Noah's people to him was through the graves, whereas the enmity of Abraham's people towards him was through the stars. Both groups fashioned their idols in the images of their deities and then worshipped them, whereas the Messengers (عَلَيْهِمُ ٱلسَّلَامُ) were exclusively sent to disband polytheism and its practitioners from the earth —to cut off its causes, to destroy its temples and to conflict with its people.[101]

Connecting the continuum of the ancient ideological assault to that of later days, Ibn Taymiyyah (رَحِمَهُ ٱللَّهُ) mentions in *al Fatwā al Ḥamawiyyah al Kubrā*:

(The *Ṣabian's*) doctrine about Al-Rabb (the Lord and Creator) is that He only has attributes of negation or of possession, or that

[101] Miftāḥ Dār al-Sa'ādah, vol. 2, p. 197. Dar al Kutub al 'Ilmiyyah, Beirut.

which is considered a combination of both.[102] They are the ones al Khalīl (Allah's beloved) Ibrāhīm عَلَيْهِ السَّلَام was sent to. Ja'd adopted this from the *Ṣabian* philosophers. Likewise is the case of Abū Naṣr al Fārābī, he entered Ḥarrān and took the completion of his philosophy from the *Ṣabian* philosophers. Also, as Al Imām Aḥmad mentioned, Jahm (78-128 h.) took this from the Samniyyah — some philosophers of India who negated everything except for what is physically sensed— when he debated with them.[103]

Ibn al Qayyim (رَحِمَهُ ٱللَّهُ) even mentions that the basis of the Eastern religions branching out of ancient Brahmanism (i.e. Hinduism & Vedic religions) is from the polytheistic strand of Ṣabianism. He says:

> The origin of this way (i.e. Brahmanism) comes from the polytheistic Ṣabians who were the people of Abraham that he debated with about the falsity of polytheism, shattering their argument with his knowledge and breaking their deities with his hands, so much so that they sought to burn him alive.[104]

The Historical Legacy of Ta'ṭīl from Pharaoh to Nebuchadnezzar[105] to Hulagu[106]

Ibn al Qayyim (رَحِمَهُ ٱللَّهُ) provides a valuable schematic for navigating the course of historical events through the lens of sound creed. He briefly outlines the legacy of the *Mu'aṭṭilah*

[102] Meaning they believed that Divine Attributes can only be statements about what the Deity is not, and that positive Divine Attributes are possessions of the Deity, separate from the Deity — thus they are created entities separate from His Essence in their estimation.

[103] Majmū' al Fatāwā, vol. 5, p. 22.

[104] Ighāthah al-Lahfān, vol. 2, p. 255. Maktabah al Ma'ārif, al-Riyāḍ, KSA. Tahqiq: Muhammad Hāmid al Faqī.

[105] circa 605- c. 562 BCE.

[106] 1218-1265 CE.

(negative theologians) handed down generationally ever since the time of Pharaoh. He traces the devastation that adopting such beliefs caused the Tribe of Israel, leading to the destruction of the Holy Temple, just as it would result in the Crusades and Mongol invasions. He says (رَحِمَهُ ٱللَّهُ):

> The Malāḥidah (atheistic philosophers) from them are adherents to pure ta'ṭīl (negation of Allah's Attributes). For certainly, they negated all revealed religion; they negated the creation from having a Creator and the Perfect Divine Attributes from belonging the Creator; and they negated from the universe the truth for which it was created. So they negated from (the world) its beginning and its ma'ād (i.e. Day of Judgment), as well as its Maker and its purpose. This disease then spread amongst the nations and the sects of the negativists from them.
>
> The Pharaoh, the leader of the negators, was one of them. He brought ta'ṭīl (purely negative theology) out into implementation. He explicitly declared it, permitted it amongst his people, propagated it, and denied that his people had any God besides him. He denied that Allah (تَبَارَكَ وَتَعَالَىٰ) is above the heavens over His throne and that He actually spoke to His worshipper and Messenger Moses (عَلَيْهِ ٱلسَّلَامُ). He belied Moses in that regard and requested that his minister Hāmān erect a tower for him to be able to look at the God of Moses, as he claimed. He belied (Moses) in that and every *Jahmite* followed his example ever since.
>
> So he belied that Allah actually speaks or that Allah (تَبَارَكَ وَتَعَالَىٰ) is above His heavens ascended over His throne, separate from His creation. He gradually introduced that to his people and associates until Allah (عَزَّ وَجَلَّ) ultimately destroyed them by way of drowning, making a lesson out of them for his believing servants and making them as a deterrent for His enemies from the negators.

During the life of Moses (عَلَيْهِ ٱلسَّلَامُ) — the one whom Allah (عَزَّوَجَلَّ) spoke to — and continuing until his death, the matter remained upon monotheism, affirming Divine Attributes, and (believing that) Allah (تَبَارَكَ وَتَعَالَىٰ) spoke to His servant Moses. After that corruption permeated the Tribe of Israel: negative theology (ta'tīl) raised its head amongst them, and they inclined towards the audience of the negators, the enemies of Moses, assigning that primacy over the texts of the Torah. So Allah (تَبَارَكَ وَتَعَالَىٰ) sent against them those who removed their authority, those who deported them from their homelands and took their progeny into captivity: just as is customary of Him and is His universal way pertaining His slaves whenever they are averse to the revelation and replace it with the speech of atheists and deniers from the philosophers and others.

In the same manner, He set the Christians (i.e., the Crusaders) against the Arab lands when philosophy and speculative theology gained preeminence — once they preoccupied themselves with it. So the Christians conquered most of their land and made them their vassals. Likewise, when that appeared in the Eastern territories, He set the armies of the Tatars against them, who obliterated and conquered most of the Eastern lands. Similarly, in the end of the third and beginning of the fourth century, when the people of Irāq became preoccupied with philosophy and the studies of atheistic theology, He set the *Qirāmiṭah* and *Bāṭiniyyah* against them. They devastated the Caliph's army multiple times, overtook those performing ḥajj, and subjected them to murder and captivity. Their power became severe, and many of the elites were suspected of secretly colluding with them, including government ministers, scribes, mentors, and others. Their du'āt (appointed advocates) conquered the western lands, and they settled their House of rulership in Egypt. It was during their days that Cairo was built. They eventually overcame the Levant, the Ḥijāz, Yemen, and the Maghreb. The sermon on Baghdād's pulpit was delivered in support of them.

The point here is that when this disease entered into the Tribe of Israel, it was the cause of their destruction and loss of rulership. Then Allah (تَبَارَكَ وَتَعَالَىٰ) dispatched His servant and Messenger, His *kalimah*[107], the Messiah, the son of Mary. So he renewed the religion for them and clarified its distinguishing features. He invited them to the worship of Allah alone and to freeing themselves from novelties and false opinions. So they showed him enmity and denied him. They accused he and his mother of lies and attempted to kill him. So Allah (تَبَارَكَ وَتَعَالَىٰ) cleansed him of them and raised him unto Himself, such that they were unable to reach him with evil. Allah (تَبَارَكَ وَتَعَالَىٰ) established supporters for him, inviting to (Allah) and to His religion, until his religion became uppermost above those who had opposed him and kings entered into it. His call spread and the matter remained upon (relative) rectitude for around three centuries. The religion of Christ ultimately took to transformation and alteration until it was replaced and vanished. Nothing of it remains in the hands of the Christians. **Instead, they synthesized another religion between the religion of Christ and the religion of the idol-worshipping philosophers.** In doing so, they attempted to simplify things for the nations so that they would enter into Christianity.[108]

Ṣabian Syncretism & the Rise of the Greek Philosophers

The aforementioned syncretic tradition resulted in an incremental wholesale merging of creeds built upon pessimism, hopelessness, and harboring bad thoughts about the creator that formed the basis for Greek philosophy. Of the utmost

[107] His word: meaning that Jesus عَلَيْهِ ٱلسَّلَامُ was created miraculously without having a father. Allah said "be" and he was. Then Jesus عَلَيْهِ ٱلسَّلَامُ was made to speak in the cradle to exonerate his mother from the slander of the Jews.

[108] Ighāthah al-Lahfān, vol. 2, pp. 268-270.

importance, central to the theme of this book, is the recognition of Greek philosophy for what it is: rationalized pagan mysticism. Undoubtedly, the historical record leaves us with no reservations as to the fact that the two most profound and formative influences on Greek philosophy were of the Iranian-Persian and the Egyptian varieties of paganism. Greek philosophy developed under these influences during the few centuries between the Persian colonization of Greece and Egypt until the Age of Alexander. The history of Greek philosophy essentially occupies a few centuries starting with Thales[109] and Anaximander,[110] and then passes through the duration of the Greco-Persian Wars and its humiliating aftereffects, until arriving at the time of Plato[111] and his pupil Aristotle,[112] the mentor of Alexander. As is known, Alexander's worldwide conquests resulted in an unprecedented surge of religious syncretism — merging the mystical beliefs of multiple pagan cultures throughout his vast empire.

The middle of this formative period of Greek philosophy coincided with the rise of Zoroastrianism (the religion of the Majus) as the official state religion of Persia. During this period the Persians waged war against Greece and many of their ideas were merged with those of Greek thought. In reference to the strongest influences on Greek philosophy — by way of Mesopotamia and Persia — Ibn al Qayyim (رَحِمَهُ ٱللَّهُ) connects between the traditional syncretism of the *Ṣabians*, dating back the people of Ibrahim, and the later rise of the Greek philosophers. He says while discussing the contending religions in the world during the advent of Islam in Arabia:

---

[109] c. 624 – c. 546 BCE.

[110] c. 610 – c. 546 BCE.

[111] c. 423 – 348 BCE.

[112] 384–322 BCE.

The Ṣabians and Philosophers: As for the heretical Ṣabians and atheistic philosophers, then they do not believe in Allah, His angels, His scripture, His messengers, or in eventually meeting Him. They do not believe in the world's beginning or the Judgment. They do not see the world as having a Lord who actively chooses what He wills, having power over and knowing all things, commanding, forbidding, dispatching messengers, revealing scripture, rewarding the righteous, and punishing the wicked. Their lot has nothing of belief except nine constellations, ten intellects, four poles and a chain connecting all of creation that more closely resembles a sequence of insanity than logical possibility... As for the Ṣabians, then they are the people of Ḥarrān, and many of them live in Byzantium.

Some of them accept what they approve of and what agrees with their minds from the religion of the prophets and practice it, being pleased with it for themselves. The core of their affair is that they claim to accept the attractive aspects from the adherents of different religions, not having any allegiance or disavowal for one religion or another nor having fanaticism for any religion over another. In their view, the religions are spiritual matters necessary for the greater good of the world, so it is meaningless for some to conflict with others. Instead, their good aspects and self-completing, character refining facets are adopted. For this reason, they are called Ṣabians because they took a departure from worshipping according to any religion or ascription to it.[113]

Much academic research and literature has been devoted to the subject of Iranian influence on Greek culture, and of somewhat equal interest has been the topic of the impact of the mystery religions of Egypt on Greek philosophy. One of the main features of Greek philosophy was the deification of human intellect. This was one of the main legacies that the Greek

[113] Hidāyah al Ḥayāra fi Ajwibah al Yahūd wal-Naṣārā, p. 229.

philosophers inherited from the Egyptians who taught them. Charles H. Vail said:[114]

> The earliest theory of salvation is the Egyptian theory. The Egyptian Mystery System had as its most important object, the deification of man, and taught that the soul of man if liberated from its bodily fetters, could enable him to become godlike and see the Gods in this life and attain the beatific vision and hold communion with the Immortals...[115]

We see this concept of **salvation by inner-enlightenment** undeniably present in Greek philosophy, just as it is readily found in all systems of thought and belief effected by Greek philosophy since antiquity until the modern era. The urge to escape the world and turn inwardly is a reflection of the nature of the times in which Greek philosophy developed.

As a result of constant invasion and encroachment, deep-seated cynicism became common-place amongst the masses, accompanied by the diffusion of foreign ideas and beliefs by invading nations. Eric Voegelin describes the tumultuous state of the world precipitating the rise of many new ideologies with pessimistic doctrines:

> For the cosmological civilizations of Mesopotamia, Syria, and Egypt, as well as for the peoples of the Mediterranean, the seventh century before Christ inaugurates the age of ecumenical empires. The Persian Empire is followed by the conquests of Alexander, the Diadochian empires,[116] the

[114] 1866–1924. He was an American life-long ordained universalist minister, an avid socialist activist, and a high level Freemason, with a penchant for Ancient Egyptian culture.

[115] Vail, C.H., 1909; P. 25.

[116] The result of a series of conflicts fought between Alexander the Great's generals over the rule of his vast empire after his death. These conflicts occurred between 322 and 275 BC. (wikipedia)

expansion of the Roman Empire, and the creation of the Parthian and Sassanian empires.

> The collapse of the ancient empires of the East, the loss of independence for Israel and the Hellenic and Phoenician city-states, the population shifts, the deportations and enslavements, and the interpenetration of cultures reduce men who exercise no control over the proceedings of history to an extreme state of forlornness in the turmoil of the world, of intellectual disorientation, of material and spiritual insecurity. The loss of meaning that results from the breakdown of institutions, civilizations, and ethnic cohesion evokes attempts to regain an understanding of the meaning of human existence in the given conditions of the world.[117]

As a result, the directionless nations fell into despair and charlatan human devils emerged to preach a false gospel of salvation by way of gnosis — inner knowledge, which in fact was nothing but mystical speculation and the meddling of Satan. The notion of gnostic paths of salvation, only attainable by escaping the world and reality, became a permanent fixture in many cultures and is still replete in Western thought, as many have meticulously explained.

> The phases of salvation are represented in the different sects and systems—and they vary from magic practices to mystic ecstasies, from libertinism through indifferentism to the world to the strictest asceticism—the aim always is destruction of the old world and passage to the new...The instrument of salvation is gnosis itself—knowledge. Since according to the gnostic ontology entanglement with the world is brought about by agnoia, ignorance, the soul will be able to disentangle itself through knowledge of its true life and its condition of alienness

[117] Voegelin, Eric. Science, politics and gnosticism: Two essays. Regnery Publishing, 2012. p. 24

> in this world. As the knowledge of falling captive to the world, gnosis is at the same time the means of escaping it.
>
> Self-salvation through knowledge has its own magic, and this magic is not harmless. The structure of the order of being will not change because one finds it defective and runs away from it. The attempt at world destruction will not destroy the world, but will only increase the disorder in society. The gnostic's flight from a truly dreadful, confusing, and oppressive state of the world is understandable.[118]

Since Greek philosophy emerged from this foreboding abyss, then the elite promise of salvation by inner-knowledge and the accompanying escapism engaged in by the Greek philosophers was no different than what is described above. Cornford, the translator of Plato's Republic, writes:

> There is a real continuity between the earliest rational speculation and the religious representation that lays behind it...Philosophy inherited from religion certain great conceptions, for instance, the ideas of God, Soul, Destiny, and Law—**which continued to circumscribe the movements of rational thought and determine their direction.**[119]

As we have already highlighted, the pagan concepts of God, Soul, Destiny, and Law were based upon: (1) a pessimistic outlook towards the Creator that resulted in ta'ṭīl (rejection of Divine Attributes for the Creator) and shirk (polytheism); (2) discounting Divine Providence and the concept of destiny; and (3) pitting reason against revealed religion, piecing together beliefs, morals, and laws for social governance according to whim. So it was in fact this attitude 'continued to circumscribe the movement of rational thought and determine (its) direction.' The mystical,

---

[118] ibid. p. 26.

[119] Cornford p. vii

pagan, mythological understandings of God, Soul, Destiny, and Law that were found in Greek religious thought were simply repurposed, rationalized, and serviced with a shift in semantics by the Greek philosophers. Or in other words, Greek philosophy is rationalized pagan mysticism.

Cornford's study documents the process of the development of Greek philosophy from its ancient religious influences to its final product. He thoroughly proves from its source material how it originated in idolatry and sorcery, only to ultimately return back to those very-same origins. The latter formative period of Greek philosophy, spanning the time between Pythagoras and Plato was cloaked in magic and pantheism. In the conclusion of his detailed study, Cornford summarizes his findings:

> When Greek philosophy deified the speculative intellect, it made the supreme effort to work clear of all that was vague and mythical in religion, only to find that the intellect had become a deity...

He then summarizes the outcome of the earlier 'scientific tradition' of Greek philosophy saying:

> If then, reason is divine in comparison with man, the life of reason is divine in comparison with human life...The ideal for the individual then is to escape from society, as God has escaped from his functional utility in Nature. Man's soul rises...above his social group. He will withdraw, like the Stoic, into autonomous self-sufficiency and Olympian contemplation.

Then he summarizes the final stage of Greek philosophy —the mystic tradition—saying:

> It is only a step further to the mystical trance of Neoplatonism,[120] in which thought is swallowed up in the beatific vision of the absolute One, above being and above knowledge, ineffable, unthinkable, no longer even a Reason, but beyond Reason — 'the escape of the alone to the alone.' In this ecstasy, Thought denies itself; and **Philosophy, sinking to the close of her splendid curving flight, folds her wings and drops into the darkness whence she arose — the gloomy Erebus[121] of theurgy and magic.**[122]

The above statement is an admission that is generally agreed upon by those who specialize on the subject of the history of philosophy. It alludes to how the deification of human reason had multifaceted results. First, it stripped life of meaning. Secondly, it caused the antisocial pseudo-intellectuals to narcissistically withdraw from society and view themselves as godlike. Thirdly, in an attempt to restore some meaning to life, it led the later generations of philosophers to mystic occultism and conversing with devils. Meaning that philosophy simply returned back to its ancient origins as had been practiced in the Mesopotamia and Egypt mystery religions. Their additional contribution to ancient mystic paganism would have a lasting impact, as the conclusion of this chapter highlights.

Chapter Conclusion: the Pagan Concept of the Logos

The central concept behind Man's deification in Greek philosophy is the idea of the ***logos***. This idea was presented with different constructions within the two traditions of Greek

[120] Neoplatonism is a philosophical school of thought following Plato's teachings as interpreted by Plotinus (c. 204/5 – 270 ce). Their doctrine is one of monism (a belief in the oneness of existence, i.e. God, Nature, and Man being of one substance).

[121] Erubus: deep darkness.

[122] ibid.

philosophy, meaning, in philosophy's scientific and mystic variations. The Encyclopedia Brittanica defines it as follows, "Logos, (Greek: "word," "reason," or "plan") plural logoi, in Greek philosophy and theology, **the divine reason implicit in the cosmos, ordering it and giving it form and meaning**."[123] As alluded to above, the ancient origins of Greek philosophy and its final product were steeped in the paganism, occultism, and magic of Greek mythology and its pantheon of false deities. This point helps us to better understand the intent of the philosophers behind this concept of the logos. It is essential to know that Greek philosophy went through two main stages of development in the period between its ancient origins and its final product, as has been mentioned. The first is called the scientific tradition, and the later is called the mystic tradition. Both traditions had a version of the concept of logos as a central theme and both would leave a lasting impact on Western thought.

This eventual impact of these traditions on Judaism and Christianity is summarized by the following statement:

> Western culture is based on the twin pillars of **Greek rationality**, on the one hand, and **biblical faith**, on the other. Certainly, there can be little doubt that these two traditions have been dominant forces in cultural development. The former may be defined by its sole reliance on the rationality of the mind, the latter by its emphasis on an authoritative divine revelation. **However, from the first centuries to the present day there has also existed a third current**, characterized by a resistance to the dominance of either pure rationality or doctrinal faith. **The adherents of this tradition emphasized the importance of inner-enlightenment or gnosis**: a revelatory experience that mostly entailed an encounter with one's true self as well as with the ground of being, God.

123 123 Encyclopedia Britannica. https://www.britannica.com/topic/logos

In order to understand what happened to 'biblical religion' then we must identify the driving force behind the 'Greek rationality' of the scientific tradition and the gnostic 'inner-enlightenment' of the mystic tradition. The answer will unravel the mystery of exactly how Christianity was later paganized.

The Earlier Rationalistic, 'Scientific' Tradition

The earlier scientific tradition of Greek philosophy served to repurpose pagan religious ideas from neighboring cultures about God, Soul, Destiny, and Law and repurposed these concepts in scientific terms, many of which are still in use today. In essence, the scientific tradition took the pagan practice of assigning divine attributes to mythical deities one step further. Having already fully denigrated the Creator and reassigned most of His Attributes to mythical beings, they proceeded to deify Nature and matter, and, by extension, the human intellect. Cornford summarizes the essence of Greek philosophy's earlier scientific tradition:

> We see that although it goes the whole way to the extreme of 'materialism,' the properties of immutability and impenetrability ascribed to atoms are the last degenerate forms of divine attributes.[124]

However, the scientific tradition did not merely settle for deifying nature, but rather it endeavored one step further. It rendered Man as a god over nature. Their skewed logic asserted that by Man using speech ***(logos)*** to name and classify Nature, he secured control over it for his own advantage and progress.

---

[124] Cornford, Francis. From Religion to Philosophy.

Through this reasoning, the attribute of Divine Will, which is seen as an obstacle to human progress, is transferred entirely onto human beings.

> Science, with its practical impulse (which is to control nature), is like magic in attempting to direct control over the world, whereas religion interposes between desire and its end an uncontrollable and unknowable factor—the will of a personal God.[125]

Meaning that the scientific tradition saw the will of God as an interference between human will and human progress.

> The perpetual, if unconscious, aim of science is to avoid this circuit though the unknown (i.e., Divine Will), and to substitute for religious representation, involving this arbitrary factor, a closed system ruled throughout by necessity.[126]

In brief, the scientific tradition of Greek philosophy aimed at exchanging belief in Divine Will and Providence for one of human control of the world, believing it to be purposeless and lifeless until Man assigns it meaning and utility. This assignment of utility and purpose happens by way of using speech (logos) to classify and describe nature. This concept of the logos as the chief deity of atheistic scientist philosophers would go through one final phase in Greek thought.

This deification of nature, and by extension the human mind, was a natural progression of centuries of misguidance. We saw earlier in this chapter how *Ṣabianism* and its syncretic counterpart of Vedic polytheism was an ancient source of worshipping nature with the Sun as a chief diety. Ibn al Qayyim رَحِمَهُ ٱللَّهُ states:

---

[125] ibid.

[126] ibid.

> This is an ancient way in the world and its adherents are diverse groups. Some of them worship the sun, claiming that it is one of the angels, having a self and intellect, and being the source of moonlight and starlight. They view all lower entities to originate from it and they say it rules the galaxy, therefore it deserves veneration, prostration, and supplication.[127]

Elsewhere he says:

> The polytheist *Ṣabians* worshipfully venerate the brightest planets and the twelve constellations and replicate them as images in their temples. The (seven) planets have specially designated temples, which are the larger houses of worship, quite similar to the churches of Christians and Synagogues of Jews. They have a large temple devoted to the sun, a temple for the moon, a temple for Venus, a temple for Jupiter, a temple for Mars, a temple for Mercury, a temple for Saturn, and a temple for the chief diety (called the the original maker).[128]

It is quite significant that the modern 'scientific revolution' from the 'Renaissance' to the 'Enlightenment' was unmistakably inspired by occultist beliefs traceable to these same mysterious ancient doctrines of the Ṣabians and the cosmological civilizations. They religiously believed that these doctrines were the guaranteed cause of the civilizational rise and linear progress for humankind. The utopian humanists of modernity sought to dethrone the concept of Providence and to enthrone Man and human progress as the new supreme deity.

Since they believed that he could only rise to divinity by way of mastering modern science, they endeavored to dethrone Man's privileged traditional view of himself and the world he lived,

---

[127] Ighāthah al-Lahfān vol. 2, p. 223.

[128]ibid. vol. 2, p. 250.

utilizing science to this end. Take as a prime example their religious belief in heliocentrism,[129] popularized by the Catholic occultist Nicolaus Copernicus[130] who writes:

> In the middle of all sits Sun enthroned. In this most beautiful temple could we place this luminary in any better position from which he can illuminate the whole at once? He is rightly called the Lamp, the Mind, the Ruler of the Universe: Hermes Trismegistus names him the Visible God, Sophocles' Electra calls him the All-seeing. So the Sun sits as upon a royal throne ruling his children, the planets, which circle round him.[131]

As you see, the 'modern' philosophers had not deviated far from the beliefs of their ancient masters. The natural philosophers' (who were later called natural scientists) denigration of man came full circle centuries later when the theory of evolution pronounced that Man is simply an intelligent ape — an advanced primate. This denigration was further accompanied by a slew of racialist implications found in Darwin's theory of 'natural selection,' contributing to the dehumanization inherent in the social Darwinist concept of the 'survival of the fittest'. Scientism and Social Darwinism would become the driving engine of colonization, as is discussed in the second volume of this work.

The utopian philosopher is the open enemy of the idea of Divine Providence and Authority over the universe. The inevitability of uncertainty — presented by belief in Divine Will — is highly offensive to the utopian because, in his mind, it

---

[129] the belief that the universe revolves around the sun. It later was later updated to believing in the galaxy revolving around the sun.

[130] Nicolaus Copernicus (19 February 1473 – 24 May 1543) was a Renaissance-era mathematician and astronomer who formulated a model of the universe that placed the Sun rather than the Earth at the center of the universe. (wikipedia)

[131] Kuhn, The Copernican Revolution, p. 131.

prevents the planning of a perfect society. They shamelessly proclaim that since God cannot be relied upon, then humankind must unite to take fate into their own hands in order to progress as a species. They believe that mankind's concern for personal salvation and devotion to God prevents each person from giving himself entirely to the common task of human progress: they conclude that God's very existence prevents mankind from establishing a fully rational and secularized society.

Their solution is the deification of humanity to carry out the common task of human progress, because this would liberate the extra energy being spent outside the human enterprise, and would channel the loyalty of man towards the planning and constructing of a worldly society. "The resulting network would be the highest achievement in the universe and credited to man as sole creator."[132] However, far from being a guarantee of social progress, history has proven without doubt that the occult based beliefs of the ancients and the moderns were the driving force behind untold misery. They forgot Allah, and so He caused them to forget themselves.

The Final, Mystic Tradition of Greek Philosophy

If one were to be intrigued enough to inquire as to whether or not the aforementioned channeling and summoning of devils that was found in the ancient systems that deified nature was also passed on by the Greeks, then the historical record answers emphatically in the affirmative. Just as the earlier scientific tradition had declared Nature as divine, as did the ancients, then the demonic, magical, mystical elements of the ancients would not be lost either. Just as the scientific tradition of Greek

[132] Molnar, Thomas. (1972) Utopia, the Perennial Heresy, p. 83.

philosophy declared Man to be Nature's master by merit of speech and reason ('logos'), thereby deifying the speculative intellect, then likewise the later, mystic phase of Greek philosophy attempted the same. The mystic tradition of Greek philosophy arose mostly to inject emotional vigor into the same concept of the 'logos' by which the scientific tradition had rendered life meaningless and soulless. In an entirely different way, they reached the same nonsensical conclusion as the scientific tradition, which was the ascription of divine attributes to man.

The first person known to promote the mystical tradition — which also placed the logos at its center — was Heracleitus in the sixth century BCE. The Encyclopedia Brittanica asserts that he was the first who was known to introduce the more popular understanding of the concept of the logos, the one that was later borrowed and adapted by the Christians:

> **(Heracleitus) discerned in the cosmic process a *logos* analogous to the reasoning power in man**. Later, the Stoics, philosophers who followed the teachings of the thinker Zeno of Citium (4th–3rd century BCE), defined the logos as an active rational and spiritual principle that permeated all reality. They called the logos providence, nature, god, and the soul of the universe, which is composed of many seminal logoi that are contained in the universal logos.

This mystic tradition ultimately became the dominant philosophical tradition and formed the basis of the teachings of Pythagoras[133] and Plato. Cornford explains that centuries before them, Herecleitus had taught that: "It is wisdom to confess that all things are one" and that "all things come out of one, and out of

[133] *c.* 580–500 BCE, Greek philosopher; known as Pythagoras of Samos. Pythagoras sought to interpret the entire physical world in terms of numbers and founded their systematic and mystical study. He is best known for the theorem of the right-angled triangle.

one all things." As such, the mystical tradition of Greek philosophy was premised upon pantheism, the doctrine identifying God with the universe, and the universe as a manifestation of God, whose attributes they believed were separate entities apart from Himself.

They called this imagined mystical, unifying commonality between all things the ***logos,*** believing that any appearance of difference or separateness in the world only 'seems' to be so while, in fact, everything is 'one' and the same. They say that 'God', Nature, Man, and Society are in fact one single thing. This pantheistic belief would later resurface in the concept of the Christian trinity, as the next chapter discusses.

> We encounter here, as we should expect, the mystical belief that the One can pass out of itself into the manifold, and yet retain its oneness...From the unity of the real follows the inevitable condemnation of the many to comparative reality or 'seeming'... There is one logos, one reason for everything, throughout 'the one cosmos, which is the same for all.' Of this one meaning all particular things are merely symbols.[134]

In other words, these pantheist mystics believed that reality is illusion and that the universe is unified by a force referred to as the *logos*:

> To the mysticism of all ages, the visible world is a myth, a tale half true and half false, embodying a logos, the truth of which is one. What, then, is the one truth, the one reality which runs through all these manifold transformations?... It is God, who is 'day and night , winter and summer, war and peace, surfeit[135] and

[134] Cornford. From Religion to Philosophy.

[135] an excessive amount of something: *a surfeit of food and drink*.

> hunger; only, he takes various shapes...What is really constant, throughout all the transformations is Logos...[136]

So logos was a false deity premised upon centuries of pagan beliefs. They believed this so-called ***logos*** to be the force balancing, proportioning, and harmonizing all things.

> This maintenance of measure, or constancy of proportion, is the principle of Justice...This Justice or Harmony is the Logos, the Spirit of Life, observing measure, but passing all barriers. It is the divine soul-substance, whose life consists in movement and change. It is also the one divine Law, the law of Nature, which is the Will of God...This is true for the universe, no less than for human society; it is common to all things...[137]

The chain of transmission for this pagan mystical concept would eventually jump many centuries forward from the days of Heracleitus and the mystic tradition of Greek philosophy to later usage by influential Hellenized Jews, such as Saul of Tarsus and Philo of Alexandria. "Inspired by the *Timaeus* of Plato, Philo read the Jewish Bible as teaching that God created the cosmos by his Word (logos), the first-born son of God."[138]

Drawing from Philo's teachings, the early Church fathers would use the concept of *logos* to fully paganize the teachings of Jesus (عَلَيْهِ الصَّلَاةُ وَالسَّلَامُ).

> Though the concept defined by the term logos is found in Greek, Indian, Egyptian, and Persian philosophical and theological systems, **it became particularly significant in**

[136] Conrnford. From Religion to Philosophy.

[137] ibid., pp. 187-192.

[138] Tuggy, Dale, "Trinity", *The Stanford Encyclopedia of Philosophy* (Winter 2016 Edition), Edward N. Zalta (ed.), URL = <https://plato.stanford.edu/archives/win2016/entries/trinity/>.

> **Christian writings and doctrines to describe or define the role of Jesus Christ as the principle of God active in the creation and the continuous structuring of the cosmos and in revealing the divine plan of salvation to man.** It thus underlies the basic Christian doctrine of the preexistence of Jesus.[139]

It is quite amazing that a concept rooted in a bewildering sludge of paganism, atheistic philosophy, and mysticism would eventually be placed at the center of Pauline Christianity despite its clear contradiction to the core fundamentals of faith. How exactly this took place is explored in the next chapter.

---

139 Encyclopedia Britannica. https://www.britannica.com/topic/logos

The Tribulation of the Antichrist

The marriage between philosophy, science, and occultist influences that combined during the development of Greek philosophy and exists in one form or another until today is one of great historical importance. The most unlikely and unexpected place to initiate an analysis of history is at its very end. As Muslims, we have this unique vantage point extended to us by Allah's mercy. The moral of the story of the Antichrist—as collected at length throughout the authentic narrations of Allah's Messenger—serves as a solid foundation of what is necessary to maintain and safeguard sound religion, despite all odds. Shaykh al Islām Ibn Taymiyyah (رَحِمَهُ ٱللَّهُ) said in *Al-Sabīniyyah*:

> Since the Antichrist's claim to Lordship is thoroughly an impossibility, then what accompanies him of miraculous feats is not a proof of his veracity; instead, it will have been a trial and test by which Allah misleads whom He wills and guides whom He wills—comparable to the (golden) calf and other (instances). However, it is the most significant trial, and his trial is not exclusively for those during his time. Instead, **the reality of his trial is that of falsehood at odds with revealed religion while accompanied by miraculous feats. Whoever concedes to what opposes the revelation because of a paranormal act has been stricken with a variation of this tribulation.** This occurs a great deal in every place and time; however, this specified individual has the most terrible trial. So long as Allah spares His servant from this — regardless of whether he (actually) encounters him (i.e., the Dajjāl) —then he will have been saved from whatever is less than this tribulation...

Commenting on the above statement, 'Abd al-Raḥmān b, Nāṣir Al-Sa'dī (رَحِمَهُ ٱللَّهُ) explains:

> I say that this benefit mentioned by the Shaykh perfectly explains how it is that the Prophet (صَلَّى ٱللَّهُ عَلَيْهِ وَسَلَّمَ) commanded his nation to seek refuge with Allah from the tribulation of the Antichrist. The reason for this is that every person direly needs to do so just as he needs Allah to grant him refuge from the punishment of the grave, from the tribulation of hellfire, and from the trial of life and death. **The "tribulation of the Antichrist" is a term denoting a category; so the worshipper must seek refuge in Allah from every tribulation of the same type as his trial—which is the tribulations of falsehood and ambiguities accompanied by doubts and miraculous acts resulting in many people's misguidance.** This is similar to the tribulation of atheism and that of the materialists by whom many are duped upon witnessing of industrial might, sensational inventions, and the likes. Ultimately, they assume that these people must be upon the truth. **This inauthentic 'civilization' that is aesthetically adorned in beauty while being internally devastated astounds them. So seeking Allah's refuge from the tribulation of the antichrist is inclusive of these sorts of trials and anything like them.**
>
> What the Shaykh mentioned answers the question as to how the Prophet (صَلَّى ٱللَّهُ عَلَيْهِ وَسَلَّمَ) could have commanded his nation to supplicate for protection from the tribulation of the antichrist, despite (the Ummah) comprising of multiple generations who would never personally encounter him. The reply to that is that every person in every time and place needs Allah's protection from the Antichrist's tribulation. And Allah knows best.[140]

[140] Al-Sa'dī. Risālatān fī fijnah al-Dajjāl wal Y'ajūj wal M'ajūj

A Transition from Monotheism & Rational Simplicity in Creed to Polytheism & Mythical Mystery

The history of Christian doctrine and Western thought is a microcosm of the tribulation described above. The mystical philosophy that subverted the original teachings meet this exact description of the Antichrist's tribulation: **falsehood and ambiguities accompanied by doubts and miraculous feats resulting in many people's misguidance.** Ibn al Qayyim says in his response to the Christians:

> The Muslims believe in the true Messiah who brought guidance and the religion of truth from Allah, the one who was Allah's servant and Messenger and who was His word which he cast to the faithful virgin Mary. The Christians only believe in a Messiah that called others to worship of himself and his mother, and to (a belief in him) being part of a trinity, either being Allah Himself or Allah's son. If such a person existed, then he would be the brother of the Antichrist. **In reality, the Christians are the followers of this false messiah, just as the Jews are anticipating his emergence while claiming to be waiting for that Prophet about whom they received glad tidings.** After he (i.e. Jesus عَلَيْهِ الصَّلَاةُ وَالسَّلَام) had already come, Satan exchanged (correct) belief in him with anticipation of the antichrist. This is the case of everyone who turns in aversion to the truth, that he has it exchanged with falsehood.[141]

Recall from the previous chapter the statement of Ibn al Qayyim about the simple monotheist, unitarian message of the Christ. He says:

> (Jesus) (عَلَيْهِ السَّلَام) invited them to the worship of Allah alone and to freeing themselves from these novelties and false opinions (i.e.

141 Ibn Qayyim al Jawziyyah. Hidāyah al Ḥayārā, p. 243.

the misinterpretations of their rabbis and the influences of the encapsulating pagan cultures). So they showed him enmity and belied him. They accused he and his mother of calumnies and attempted to kill him. So Allah (تَبَارَكَ وَتَعَالَىٰ) cleansed him of them and raised him unto Himself, such that they were unable to reach him with evil. Allah (تَبَارَكَ وَتَعَالَىٰ) established supporters for him, inviting to (Allah) and to His religion, until his religion became uppermost above those who had opposed him and until some kings entered into it. **His call spread and the matter remained upon (relative) correctness for around three centuries. The religion of the Messiah ultimately took to transformation and alteration until it was replaced and vanished. Nothing of it remains in the hands of the Christians. Rather they synthesized another religion between the religion of the Messiah (عَلَيْهِ ٱلسَّلَامُ) and the religion of the idol-worshipping philosophers. By doing so, they attempted to simplify things for the nations so that they would enter into Christianity.**[142]

Ibn al Qayyim has summarized above what is commonly referred to as the early history of the Church and the Christianization of paganism. The average Christian may dismiss the above statement as an exercise in polemics, however even Tertullian,[143] the first Church father to introduce the term Trinity, admitted that among the Christians of his day "the common people think of Christ as a man."[144] The first edition of the Encyclopedia Americana states that this simple monotheistic belief, "in some form and of varying degree has accompanied Christianity from the beginning, at least as one of its forms."[145] Furthermore, it states that the least that could be said about the

---

[142] Ighāthah al-Lahfān, vol. 2, pp. 268-270.

[143] c. 155 – c. 240 AD

[144] The Encyclopedia Americana, 1918-1920. Vol. 1, p. 293.

[145] ibid.

development of the early Church's theology is that "it is usually conceded that even though it might not be correct to speak of Christianity during the first two or three centuries as being substantially Unitarian, it at least was not Trinitarian."[146] In similar fashion, The Encyclopedia Britannica states that the Unitarians were existent "at the beginning of the third century still forming the large majority."[147] A more updated edition of the Encyclopedia Americana states that:

> Unitarianism as a theological movement began much earlier in history; **indeed it antedated Trinitarianism by many decades**. Christianity derived from Judaism, and Judaism was strictly Unitarian. **The road which led from Jerusalem to the Council of Nicaea was scarcely a straight one.** Fourth-century Trinitarianism did not reflect accurately early Christian teaching regarding the nature of God; it was on the contrary a deviation from this teaching.[148]

The historical record is replete with examples of how extremely crooked the road was from Jesus' Jerusalem to the Council of Nicaea. Jan Jangeneel, the Dutch Reformist academic and missionary stated, "In the course of the first centuries of the Common Era, Christianity was shaped and reshaped by church leaders, theologians, martyrs, monks, missionaries, Bible translators, painters, and builders of churches and monasteries."[149] More specifically, in what follows, we identify how the syncretic blending of pagan mysticism and philosophy with revealed religion drastically transformed the latter until it was palatable to and assimilated by the encapsulating pagan

---

[146] ibid.

[147] Encyclopedia Britannica , 11th ed., Vol. 23, 963.

[148] *Encyclopedia Americana*, 1956. 5th edition, Vol. 27, p. 294.

[149] Jongeneel, JAB. Jesus in World History, p. 87.

cultures. A series of events eventuated in the Christianization of the barbarian pagan nations throughout Europe, who simply merged their traditional pagan beliefs, customs, celebrations and rituals with those of Christianity, until the one was indiscernible from the other. Meaning that as pagandom was Christianized, Christianity was paganized. This is so well documented and argued in defense of by Christian writers themselves throughout history that it really does not require great elaboration. Ibn al Qayyim (رَحِمَهُ ٱللَّهُ) said:

> Once Christian scholars and monks saw that the Greeks and Romans were polytheist and as such it would be difficult to convert them to pure monotheism, **they fashioned for them a religion that was a composite of both the Prophets' religion and the associationists' religion**. The Greeks and Byzantines worshipped idols that were statues casting shadows, so the Christians, in turn, incorporated shadowless icons designed into walls and roofs. Whereas (the pagans) used to prostrate in worship to the Sun and Moon, the Christians ended up prostrating towards it and replaced prostrating in worship for it with prostrating towards it (as a prayer direction).[150]

The most impactful of such changes that reshaped the teachings of the Messiah trace back to the opportunistic 'conversions' of two people centuries apart, parenthesizing the development of paganism in the early Church: the first is the conversion of Saul of Tarsus (10 - c. 63 CE), known thereafter as Paul the apostle to the Gentiles; the second is that of the Roman emperor Constantine (272–337 CE). No-one adequately familiar with history can doubt that these were the two most formative conversions and influences in early Christianity. Both were predicated upon claims of mystical visions, and both precipitated alterations bearing ramifications that would forever change Jesus' teachings and consequently would change the world.

---

150 Ibn Qayyim al Jawziyyah. Ighātha al-Lahfān fī Maṣā'id al-Shayṭān, Vol. 2, p. 270.

Ibn Taymiyyah comments on the events of Constantine's and Paul's conversion stories in light of similar events. He quotes and then comments on an important verse from the Quran about the meddling of the devils, elaborating on instances similar to these two aforementioned mystical encounters:

﴿ هَلْ أُنَبِّئُكُمْ عَلَىٰ مَن تَنَزَّلُ الشَّيَاطِينُ تَنَزَّلُ عَلَىٰ كُلِّ أَفَّاكٍ أَثِيمٍ ﴾

"[221.] Shall I inform you (O people!) upon whom the *Shayatin* (devils) descend? [222.] They descend on every lying, sinful person."[151]

> It has been transmitted in the gospels that some of the disciples saw the one who was crucified and buried in the grave stand from the grave after being buried. They saw him twice or thrice, and he showed them the site of the nails and said: Do not think me to be a devil. If they genuinely saw this, then that was a devil claiming to be the Messiah, and these people were confused. Similar things had happened to many people in our time and before it, such as some people who were in Tadmur (Palmyra, Syria) that saw an enormous figure flying in the air. He appeared to them on multiple occasions with different garments and told them that he was the Messiah, the son of Mary. He commanded them to do things that the Messiah would not order to be done. He held audience with some people who then clarified to the others that he was was nothing but a devil desiring to mislead them.
>
> There were others who went to the graves of righteous persons or others who they revered and held in high regard. Sometimes they would find the vault open, after which a person would exit with that man's appearance. Sometimes they would see that person entering a tomb. Sometimes they would see him riding or walking, entering the place of the deceased, such as the domed mausoleums. Sometimes they would see him exiting that location and imagine him to be that specific righteous man. He

[151] Al-Shu'arā': 221-222.

might think that some people are seeking his deliverance by prayer and would go to them. That would be a devil assuming his appearance... Similar occurrences happen to many polytheists and Christians, as they do for many Muslims. One of them will see a Shaykh who they have high regard for, who will tell them that he is Shaikh so-and-so, while in fact being a devil...

Similarly, what Constantine saw of the cross that he saw in the zodiac, and the cross that he saw in another instance was something fashioned by devils, who showed them that to mislead them. This is similar to what the Devils have done to a more significant degree with the idolaters. Similarly, there are those who mentioned that the Messiah came to them while awake and addressed them with some issues, as is said about Paul. If he was truthful about that, then the entity he saw while awake that informed him that it was the Messiah, was one of the devils, just as has taken place with many others. Satan only misguides people and sets them astray through that which he thinks they will comply with him pertaining. So he addresses the Christians with that which agrees to their religion just as he converses with misguided Muslims with that which conforms to their creed.[152]

Let us then look at the stories of Constantine's and Paul's mystical encounters that flung the syncretic doors of philosophy, allegorical interpretation, and speculative theology wide open ever since.

Constantine

As for Constantine's mystical vision and its aftermath, then it is a legend shrouded in mystery and myth. In the year 312, at the Battle of Milvian Bridge, During his bloody quest to consolidate his rule and secure the title of Emperor, Constantine claimed to have had a mystical epiphany, very similar to Paul's vision on the

[152] Ibn Taymiyyah. Al Jawāb al-Ṣaḥīḥ, Vol. 2, pp. 317-324.

road to Damascus hundreds of years beforehand. The Bishop Eusebius relates that Constantine personally narrated this event to him. He writes:

> He said that about noon, when the day was already beginning to decline, he saw with his own eyes the trophy of a cross of light in the heavens, above the sun, and bearing the inscription, CONQUER BY THIS. At this sight he himself was struck with amazement, and his whole army also, which followed him on this expedition, and witnessed the miracle.[153]

Constantine's questionable conversion eventuated in the arbitrary imposition of the trinitarian Nicaean creed (325 CE), by which he effectively anointed the pagan doctrine of the the mystical Alexandrian school with State sanctioned officialdom. The political opportunism of Constantine's conversion is paper-thin in its transparency: with Constantine's conversion, Christianity went from being the religion of a persecuted pacifistic minority waiting for a savior king, to that of a militarized tool of empire, consolidating power for the new Emperor over an enormous swath of territory. A number of historians concur that "Constantine, like his father, worshipped the Unconquered Sun [Sol Invictus]... His conversion should not be interpreted as an inward experience of grace... It was a military matter."[154] After his conversion the Church extolled him as Constantine, the Great, Equal to the Apostles. Even when trying to portray his conversion in the best light, Church theologians provide extremely awkward explanations, such as the following:

> We know for certain that Constantine was exposed to monotheism and religious tolerance from an early age by way of his father, Constantius, whom he emulated in many ways.

---

[153] Eusebius of Caesarea. The Life of the Blessed Emperor Constantine, Chapter XXVIII.

[154] Chadwick, Henry. The Early Church, (1993) pp. 122-125.

> Constantius was a strict adherent to Sun-God worship and Constantine, having considered the systematic failure of those who practiced polytheism,"felt it incumbent on him to honor his father's God alone".[155] And according to Lactantius, Constantine consistently followed his father's use of tolerant policy towards Christianity from his proclamation as Augustus.[156]

How mind-boggling is it that a Christian would consider Sun-worship as a monotheistic practice?! But this is a necessary mental construct to assert that Constantine was following the 'monotheistic' example of his father, as opposed to others who have aptly pointed out that Constantine merely switched one form of paganism for another for political expediency. In reality, once again the zodiac worshipping Ṣabian elements from Ḥarrān had corrupted revealed religion, forevermore changing Christianity through Constantine. Ibn Taymiyyah al Ḥarrānī (رَحِمَهُ ٱللَّٰهُ) explains:

> When a group of the people of Ḥarrān entered Christianity, notably amongst them was Helena from the Fandaqāniyyah neighborhood of Ḥarrān. Constantine's father, who at the time was the Roman emperor, fell in love with her and then married her, after which she gave birth to Constantine. She converted her son Constantine to Christianity who then gave preeminence to the Christian religion and built Constantinople.
>
> During his time, the Christians innovated the (Nicaean) Creed that their various sects agree upon today. Around three hundred and ten scholars and monks unanimously conceded to it. They say that it was he who innovated prayer toward the

---

[155] as stated by Eusebius.

[156] Hardenbrook, V.R.F.T., Emperor Constantine the Great (306–337). The Importance of His Faith in the History of the Church.

east, prior to which not a single Prophet or any of their followers prayed towards the east.[157]

Paul the 'Apostle to the Heathens'

As for Paul's mystical vision and its aftermath, then Paul claims that before spreading his divergent version of Christology, he was under the authority of the High Priest[158] and had been killing and capturing believers in Jesus (عَلَيْهِ السَّلَامُ) city by city. On his way to Damascus, he claimed to have a mystic vision during which he ascended into the third heaven and spoke directly to Jesus. This mysterious encounter cloaked him with the enigmatic mantle of being the Apostle to the Heathen Gentiles, somehow entitling him forever after to be the most important disciple and apostle of Christ, ostensibly teaching the only official version of Christology. It is indisputable that Pauline Christianity is the earliest interpretation of Christ's teachings to which the world has access, and subsequently, it has remained the dominant Christology ever since the destruction of the Second Temple in Jerusalem in 70 CE, after which the Church systematically suppressed all significant challenges raised against his teachings.

Despite his claim of rabbinical training, Jewish academics have demonstrated that there is no real indication that he was a Hebrew scholar. Instead, he appears to have been a Hellenist[159] who introduced his version of Jesus as a salvation figure to rescue

---

[157] Ibn Taymiyyah. Al-radd 'alā-l manṭiqiyyīn, p. 289.

[158] As an important note, the High Priest was a Sadducee, the oppositional party to the Pharisees, which contradicts Paul's claim to have been a Pharisee.

[159] Hellenists: A group of Jews who read the Septuagint Greek translation of Old Testament scriptures rather than the Hebrew version. They spoke Greek rather than Aramaic. For nearly two centuries there had been an uneasy relationship between Jews who welcomed Hellenistic culture and those who defended conservative Hebrew customs and distinctions. (http://www.oxfordbiblicalstudies.com)

human souls from what he described as an evil world. Thus, his religious ideas and thoughts are closer to those of Gnosticism than those of Judaism. The Jewish Encyclopedia's entry on Saul of Tarsus by Kaufmann Kohler (1843 – 1926) bluntly rejects the claim of Paul to have received rabbinical training, by which he presented himself to his non-Jewish audience as a former Pharisee. Instead, all indicators point to his having been a Hellenist and that his claim to have had rabbinical training was simply a ploy to (1) exude an air of religious authority about himself and (2) to portray his Christology as a continuation of Jewish doctrine and scripture.

Even though Jesus (عَلَيْهِ السَّلَام), according to many passages in the Gospels, declared that he was exclusively sent to guide the lost sheep of Israel, Paul, independent of the Disciples and the original Israelite community, nominated himself to universalize his peculiar version of Christianity to all peoples. He employed guile and cunning while piecing together his own religion for mass appeal. As he famously stated: "I am made all things to all men, that I might, by all means, save some." This ploy proved to be an "ends justifying the means" Machiavellian-like loosening of truth and morality that Paul deemed necessary to accommodate the heathen masses in the Greek-speaking world. He is quoted in his epistles to have said the following,"The important thing is that in every way, whether from false motives or true, Christ is preached."[160] "If my falsehood enhances God's truthfulness, and so increases his glory, why am I still condemned as a sinner?"[161] As the Christian proverb goes, "When in Rome, do as the Romans do."

---

[160] Philippians 1:18

[161] Romans 3:7

Paul unmistakably altered Jesus's teachings by Hellenizing them in both word and meaning. He proselytized in Greek, and he instituted many mystical, pagan aberrations, taking a noticeable departure from both the Jews and early followers of Jesus. He initiated the practice of using ambiguous terms rooted in Greek philosophy and allegory to appeal to the heathen mind, and this practice would later be replicated by many of the early Church fathers, resulting in endless debates and eventuating in the trinitarian creed. Every aspect of Pauline thought went against the core of the what the Israelite Prophets were known to have taught. The Jewish academic Hyam Maccaby summarized how Paul had synthesized his new religion out of Judaism, Gnosticism and mystery religion:

> It was an imaginative creation of tremendous poetic power, and its progress in the Greco-Roman world is not to be wondered at. Its chief ingredients are indeed Greco-Roman rather Jewish, and its appeal was to the world-weary Hellenists, yearning for escape from disorientation and despair, not to the Jews... Pauline Christianity, despite its effort to anchor itself in Judaism by usurping the Jewish religion-historical scheme, is far from Judaism in tone. Its basic world attitude is that of Gnosticism, reinforced by powerful sado-masochistic [162] elements derived from mystery religion, evoking echoes of primitive sacrifice.[163]

Paul's influence would be the most impactful on Christian doctrine. "Paul fashioned a Christ of his own, a church of his own, and a system of belief of his own; and because there were many mythological and Gnostic elements in his theology which appealed more to the non-Jew than to the Jew, he won the

---

[162] sado-masochism is gratification gained through inflicting or receiving pain.

[163] Maccaby, Hyam. The mythmaker: Paul and the invention of Christianity, p. 198.

heathen world to his belief."[164] The Pauline contributions can be summarized as follows:

1. Paul replaced a natural, rational belief in an Omniscient, Omnipotent God with an alternative system of blind mystical belief. On principle, as a human is exaggerated in status and eventually assigned divine qualities, this denigrates the Creator's status — until the concept of God dissolves into deification of creation, rendering the Creator and the creation indistinguishable from each other in thought. This is an unmistakable departure from the monotheism taught by all of the Prophets. There was certainly no precedence for the teachings of the Israelite Prophets:

> Only the pagan idea of the "man-God" or "the second God," the world's artificer,[165] and "son of God", or the idea of a king of light descending to Hades, as in the Mandæan-Babylonian literature, could have suggested to Paul **the conception of a God who surrenders the riches of divinity and descends to the poverty of earthly life in order to become a savior of the human race**. Only from Alexandrian Gnosticism, or... only from pagan pantheism, could he have derived the idea of the "pleroma," "the fulness" of the Godhead dwelling in Christ as the head of all principality and power, as him who is before all things and in whom all things consist.[166]

Remember Ibn al Qayyim's previous statement that the one who assigns counterparts for Allah wittingly or unwittingly denigrates the Creator, and thus the Creator denigrates him for doing so. This is the premise of Paul's Christology: **"Throughout all the Epistles a share in the divinity is**

[164] *The Jewish Encyclopedia.*

[165] meaning its maker.

[166] Singer, I. and Adler, C. eds., 1907. *The Jewish Encyclopedia,* p. 84.

ascribed to Jesus in such a manner as to detract from the glory of God."[167]

Even beyond that, this assignment of shared divinity is extended further beyond Jesus, and made available for the community by means of particular rituals by which they ostensibly become one with Christ. "Securing a mystic union with the Deity by means of sacramental rites"[168] is a markedly heathen concept. The traditional religious laws of the Jews would be replaced by such sacraments like baptism and the Eucharist which would ostensibly join the faith community in mystic union with the Divine, teaching that (1) baptism freed them from 'original sin' thus rendering them holy, and that (2) the consumption of bread and wine in the Eucharist actually transforms into the flesh and blood of Jesus. In short, Paul's scheme reassigns a portion of divinity to his version of the Prophet and then to Paul's community of followers.

2. Ambiguous speech in some of Paul's writing denied the allowance of healthy impulses. Paul proves to be very prudish and frequently taught that the material world is evil in essence. Notably, he asserts that sexual desire and marital intimacy is disliked and better if avoided, thus enjoining celibacy on both men and woman as the preferable standard of righteousness.[169] The social implications of Paul's exhortations about marital relations, divorce, and remarrying after divorce or being widowed are very harmful. This deprivation of a natural human need resulted in the rise of monasticism, which was finally institutionalized in the mystic confines of Alexandria during the fifth century, setting an

---

[167] ibid.

[168] ibid.

[169] II Corinthians 7.

unattainable irrational, unrealistic standard for piety based on pagan influences.

3. He declared the revealed law of the Jews to be the actual cause of sin and damnation, saying that one could be saved only by Grace.[170] What does he mean by Grace? By Grace, he intends his peculiar version of Jesus as a savior. He is saying that only by assigning divinity to other than the God of the Prophets can one attain Grace. He completely dismisses the notion that individual and social ethics rest upon compliance to Divine Law. So by abolishing the Law, he ignored that Grace is received by dutifulness and compliance with divine commandments, as the Prophets had always taught. That was traditionally the standard for righteousness and the manifestation of the genuineness of faith. Such a notion is ostensibly outmoded and obsolete with Paul. It is too much for the pagan sensibilities and is a roadblock to his religion. He and his successors execrated biblical law to such a degree that it counterintuitively "led to that systematic defamation and profanation of the Old Testament and its God by Marcion and his followers[171] which ended in a Gnosticism so depraved and so shocking as to bring about a reaction in the Church in favor of the Old Testament against the Pauline antinomianism.[172]"[173]

---

[170] Ephesians 2:8–9.

[171] Marcionism was an Early Christian dualist belief system that originated in the teachings of Marcion of Sinope at Rome around the year 144. Marcion believed Jesus was the savior sent by God, and Paul the Apostle was his chief apostle, but he rejected the Hebrew Bible and the God of Israel. Marcionists believed that the Hebrew God was a separate and lower entity than the God of the New Testament. (wikipedia)

[172] antinomian: one who holds that under the gospel dispensation of grace the moral law is of no use or obligation because faith alone is necessary to salvation (Merriam-Webster.com)

[173] The Jewish Encyclopedia.

4. Just as he clashed with the Law of the Torah, he clashed with the original Disciples of Jesus, who maintained that adherence to the Law of the Torah was compulsory. A particular point of contention was the issue of circumcision for converts. Paul spews animus for those who call for adherence to the law, calling them deceivers[174] and 'dogs'[175]. He isolated himself from the disciples by avoiding being in proximity to them, spreading his message instead throughout the pagan world of Greece, Macedonia, and Asia Minor, until he ultimately situated himself in Rome until his death. "Consciously or unconsciously, he worked for a church with its world-center in Rome instead of in Jerusalem...he laid the foundation of the world-dominion of pagan Christianity."[176]

Opening the Floodgates of Allegorical Misinterpretation

There are many ambiguous phrases in Paul's epistles that are understood as allegorical, bearing a slight resemblance with Philo's sort of Gnostic teachings. It is quite fascinating and remarkable when we look at the sole instance in Paul's letters where Paul employed the actual word "allegorical". This Pauline precedent would provide the sanctioning of allegorical interpretation for the Church fathers and their successors until today.

> Paul's use of the participle (i.e., the word meaning allegory) in Galatians 4:24 has certainly attracted a wealth of commentary.

---

[174] For there are many who are insubordinate, empty talkers and deceivers, especially those of the circumcision party. Titus 1:10.

[175] Phillipians 3:2.

[176] The Jewish Encyclopedia.

> From Origen[177] to modern day New Testament scholars commentators have grappled with the meaning and intention behind Paul's use of this particular term. Origen, for example, claimed to have found in the apostle's words – at the justification for his own interpretive agenda: namely, that all of the historical narrative of Scripture is to be read allegorically.[178]

David Runia, who devoted much of academic his career to such matters, writes about this passage in his scholarly *Philo in early Christian literature*:

> It is especially interesting to trace the history of interpretation of this particular motif in the Church fathers, for the tradition gives them a choice, as it were between the Philonic and the Pauline interpretation.[179]

Since the Church fathers found no scriptural precedence for this to extrapolate exegetical method from, they were compelled to resort to its nearest approximation which could only be found in the writings of Philo of Alexandria, a mystical Hellenized Jew. Furthermore, there are two very important inquiries to be investigated here: What were the historical ramifications of Paul's practice of allegorical interpretation and its impact on Church doctrine? And what is the specific instance where Paul officially sanctioned this use of allegorical interpretation? By answering the second question we will arrive at the answer to the first:

---

[177] Origen, Latin in full Oregenes Adamantius, (born c. 185, probably Alexandria, Egypt —died c. 254, Tyre, Phoenicia [now Ṣūr, Lebanon]), the most important theologian and biblical scholar of the early Greek church. https://www.britannica.com/biography/Origen

[178] Di Mattei, Steven. "Paul's Allegory of the Two Covenants (Gal 4.21-31) in Light of First-Century Hellenistic Rhetoric and Jewish Hermeneutics." *New Testament Studies* 52, no. 1 (2006): 102-122.

[179] Runia, David T. Philo in early Christian literature: A survey. p. 86

Paul employs allegory to dismiss the biblical prophecy of Divine promise for the offspring of Abraham, meaning Isaac and Ishmael. Paul rejects that Abraham actually had two wives, Sarah and Hagar, as well as two sons, Isaac and Ishmael, for whom there was an explicit covenant and Divine Promise. As a side note, we have already seen Paul's prudish attitudes to marital intimacy and his enjoinment of monogyny. So Paul explains away Abraham's polygyny for multiple reasons. But that is not Paul's larger purpose here. Paul said that Abraham's two wives and two sons was not literal but were an allegory referring to two different covenants given by God to Jerusalem of the past and Jerusalem at Paul's time — meaning Jerusalem in bondage (like Hagar) and a free Jerusalem like Sarah). Here Paul is writing to European converts in Galatia, a European people of Celtic stock. He is blatantly discounting the biblical teaching that there is a literal Divine covenant of blessing for the Ishmaelite Arabs. By doing so, Paul redirects the European mind away from the biblical foretelling that the Ishmaelite Arabs would become a great nation by Divine blessing, something that did not and would not happen until the advent of Islam. But that is not all.

This bit of information makes it all the more interesting that Paul's main instance of heretical allegory would open up the floodgates of speculative theology and doctrinal schisms that have not closed ever since. As David Runia stated, "the tradition gives them (i.e., the Church fathers) a choice, as it were, between the Philonic and the Pauline interpretation."[180] He means that the ambiguity and vagueness of Paul's allegorical method of interpretation could only be satisfied by looking at another Hellenized Jew of a similar mystic variety as Paul — one that had employed allegory to write an exegesis of the Hebrew Scriptures. This was none other than the heretical, mystic philosopher Philo of Alexandria. We must now ask ourselves: **What exactly was**

---

[180] ibid., p. 86

the contribution to Christianity by Philo, a mystical Jew and what was the extent of its impact? — bearing in mind that "**if Philo had never existed, the interpretation of the Gospel by the Church fathers would not have been the same**."[181]

Logos: The Word of God?

Bart Ehrman writes:

> It is interesting that one of the most philosophically astute Jews of the first century, Philo of Alexandria, wrote a commentary on the book of Genesis in which he tried to show that, when properly understood, Moses stood in direct continuity with Plato. Philo himself can be understood as a Middle Platonist, taking the Middle Platonic notions of **the One supreme spiritual God and the realm of divine intermediaries between that God and this world, and applying them to his interpretation of Scripture**.[182]

Astoundingly, Philo openly proclaimed to experience mystical visions providing him with polytheistic, occultist allegorical interpretation of scripture. "Philo's results run parallel to those of mysticism and those of the Kabbalists."[183] He produced the first introduction of the concept of the Trinity as God, Word, and Wisdom. In the Stanford Encyclopedia of Philosophy it states:

> A direct influence on second century Christian theology is the Jewish philosopher and theologian Philo of Alexandria (a.k.a. Philo Judaeus) (ca. 20 BCE - ca. 50 CE), the product of

[181] ibid., p. 83

[182] Ehrman, Bart D. Lost Christianities: The battles for Scripture and the faiths we never knew. 2005. p. 120.

[183] Edersheim, Alfred (1899). *The life and times of Jesus the Messiah*. p. 50.

> Alexandrian Middle Platonism (with elements of Stoicism and Pythagoreanism). Inspired by the Timaeus of Plato, Philo read the Jewish Bible as teaching that God created the cosmos by his Word (logos), the first-born son of God. Alternately, or via further emanation from this Word, God creates by means of his creative power and his royal power, conceived of both as his powers, and yet as agents distinct from him, giving him, as it were, metaphysical distance from the material world.
>
> Another influence may have been the Neopythagorean Middle Platonist Numenius, who posited a triad of gods, calling them, alternately, "Father, creator and creature; fore-father, offspring and descendant; and Father, maker and made", or on one ancient report, Grandfather, Father, and Son. Moderatus taught a similar triad somewhat earlier.[184]

The extent of Philo's influence on the early Church Fathers and thus his influence on Christian theology was widely discussed by the clergy until the late modern era.

We have already highlighted that the driving force behind Greek philosophy was the deification of the intellect and that they arrived at this conclusion by synthesizing and rationalizing primitive paganism and the mysteries of Egypt and Mesopotamia. One of the beliefs central to Greek philosophy was that of the *Logos.* In *From Religion to Philosophy*, Francis Cornford says about the the mystic philosophers: "To the mysticism of all ages, the visible world is a myth, a tale half true and half false, embodying a logos, the truth of which is one."[185] The early philosophers asserted that logos is a cosmic process similar to the reasoning power in man. To recap the conclusion of the last chapter, the

---

[184] Tuggy, Dale, "Trinity", *The Stanford Encyclopedia of Philosophy* (Winter 2016 Edition), Edward N. Zalta (ed.), URL = <https://plato.stanford.edu/archives/win2016/entries/trinity/>.

[185] Cornford, Francis. From religion to philosophy, p. 187.

first philosopher known to coin the term *Logos* was Heracleitus. As Cornford has pointed out, Heracleitus fits squarely within the beginning of the mystic tradition of philosophy and advocated a strong belief in monism (the belief that all of existence — Creator and creation — is one single entity). He taught, "It is wisdom to confess that all things are one" and "all things come out of one, and one out of all things."[186] This is identical to the later Ṣufi belief in *waḥdah al wujūd* (the oneness of existence) that was inspired by the same influences. Cornford sums up Heracleitus's theology of the *logos* that was revived by Philo of Alexandria:

> Philo Judeaus of Alexandria taught that the logos was separate from God and was the intermediary between God and the cosmos. He asserted that it was the agent of creation and the agent by which the intellect can know God.

Not surprisingly, many of the early Church fathers "saw significant affinities between the authoritative writings of the New Testament canon and what they read in Philo's treatises."[187] For example, Justin Martyr wrote the following:

> The *Logos* is the pre-existent, absolute, personal Reason, and Christ is the embodiment of it, the Logos incarnate. Whatever is rational is Christian, and whatever is Christian is rational. The Logos endowed all men with reason and freedom, which are not lost by the fall. He scattered seeds of truth before his incarnation, not only among the Jews, **but also among the Greeks and barbarians, especially among philosophers and poets, who are the prophets of the heathen. Those who lived reasonably and virtuously in obedience to this**

[186] ibid., p. 185.

[187] Runia, David T. Philo in early Christian literature, p. 84

preparatory light were Christians in fact, though not in name.[188]

The support of the Ante-Nicean fathers[189] (specifically those of the Alexandria school) for scriptural and creedal distortions of both mystic and philosophic origin were initially introduced quite early on by both Paul and Philo. Although never professing to follow Christ, Philo's doctrine was embraced and ultimately championed by the Church fathers of Alexandria, leading to the Council of Nicaea and the ratification of the Trinitarian Nicaean Creed, three centuries later.

On a similar note, the same tendencies can be observed about many of the most influential of the Church fathers. A prime example is that of Augustine of Hippo,[190] who is seen as being the most influential Christian after Paul. His conversion from dualistic Manichean[191] materialism to Neoplatonic spirituality, and then eventually to Christianity, is symbolic of the syncretic process latent in the Roman Empire's conversion to Christianity.

---

[188] Schaff, Philip. History of the Christian Church. AD 1-311. vol. 1. p. 723. (1884).

[189] The Ante-Nicene Period (literally meaning "before Nicaea") of the history of early Christianity was the period following the Apostolic Age of the 1st century down to the First Council of Nicaea in 325. (wikipedia)

[190] St. Augustine, also called Saint Augustine of Hippo, original Latin name Aurelius Augustinus, (born November 13, 354, Tagaste, Numidia [now Souk Ahras, Algeria]—died August 28, 430, Hippo Regius [now Annaba, Algeria]; feast day August 28), bishop of Hippo from 396 to 430, one of the Latin Fathers of the Church and perhaps the most significant Christian thinker after St. Paul. Augustine's adaptation of classical thought to Christian teaching created a theological system of great power and lasting influence. (Encyclopedia Britannica) After his baptism and conversion to Christianity in 386, Augustine developed his own approach to philosophy and theology, accommodating a variety of methods and perspectives. (TeSelle, Eugene (1970). *Augustine the Theologian.* London. pp. 347–349.)

[191] Manichaeism was the religion of the pseudo-prophet Mani who taught an elaborate dualistic cosmology describing the struggle between a good, spiritual world of light, and an evil, material world of darkness. Through an ongoing process that takes place in human history, light is gradually removed from the world of matter and returned to the world of light, whence it came. Its beliefs were based on local Mesopotamian religious movements and Gnosticism. (wikipedia)

One set of pagan rites is simply reworded, repurposed, or exchanged for another, just as the Greek philosophers had done. Augustine was nothing more than a Neoplatonist mystic with a tincture of Christianity, yet his teachings are core to Christian doctrine until today. The same could be said about the Church in general from that time until now.

Gnosticism begets Gnosticism

Another influential group who were influenced by a combination of Greek thought and Pauline theology must be highlighted at this juncture. They were an influential mystical 'gnostic' elite, constituting a secretive, subversive element within the early community. Their origins trace back to two groups: first were the Jewish apocalytists,[192] who believed that the end of the world and Kingdom of God was at hand; the second influence was that of the Gnostic teachings of the Middle Platonists, who followed the teachings of Philo of Alexandria, whose influence on the trinity doctrine we have already seen. After the destruction of the Second Temple in 70 CE, many became alienated and desperate, providing fertile ground for the spread of 'gnostic' alternative paths of salvation, effectively merging these two ideologies. It is worth emphasizing that the destruction of the Second Temple also resulted in the displacement of the Jews and the significant weakening of the Nazarenes, who were the earliest community of believers in Jesus's teachings. After this incident, the only substantial Christology was the interpretation given by

[192] Jewish apocalypticism holds a doctrine that there are two eras of history: the present era, which is a combination of good and evil, and a purely good world to come that will be ruled over by God. At the time of the coming era, there will be a messiah who will deliver the faithful into the new era. Due to incidents arising very early on in Jewish history, predictions about the time of the coming of the Jewish messiah were highly discouraged, lest people lose faith when the predictions did not come true during the lifespan of the believer. (wikipedia)

Paul and his followers. It must be shown now that Paul also influenced the Gnostics, who were the most heretical opponents to those who followed Paul's interpretation in the early Church. This element strategically embedded itself into the Christian community. Far from being isolated or ostracized, the Gnostic element positioned itself fiscally and socially at the heart of the early Church at a time when its supporters were few.

Some of the most influential and heretical of the gnostics, particularly the Valentinians, claimed to follow Paul's teachings and to be initiated into the mysteries through him. Foremost researchers on this topic, such as the Princeton professor and religious historian Elaine Pagels in her book The Gnostic Paul, have highlighted clear examples of Gnostic tendencies in Pauline Christology. She concludes that Paul being a Gnostic cannot definitively be confirmed or denied. Thus the affiliation to gnosticism is enigmatic, just as was Paul. However, it is abundantly clear that Paul strongly influenced certain Gnostic sects.

According to the Gnostics, they were merely following Paul's example. The gist of the Gnostics' claims to be abiding by Paul's example is summarizable in a few points related to their interpretation of Paul's epistles: For one, they justify their elitism by citing that Paul recognized that only a few select were ready to receive the "wisdom of God hidden in a mystery." Secondly, they justified their libertarianism and licentiousness by citing Paul's antinomianism, asserting that those firm believers who have gnosis celebrate their release from the curse of the law, just as Paul dismissed the requirements of the Torah. Parallels of this permissive attitude exist with many mystical groups throughout history, stemming from ancient cults to the New Age sexual revolution. Despite Paul's prudishness, as has been highlighted, his attitude towards the moral law opened up the floodgates of licentious behavior for many heretics. Thirdly, Paul's independence of the Disciples, claiming to receive revelation directly from Jesus was used by the Gnostics to assert that other enlightened souls can experience the same.

To summarize, most of what they claim of affiliation with Paul follows these general arguments: (1) only a secret elite could fully grasp the mysteries; (2) the enlightened initiates of the gospel mysteries were liberated from the burdens of religious law; and (3) this elite was independent from any religious authority because through gnostic enlightenment, they could communicate directly with the Divine. All of these were trademark Pauline heresies.[193]

The entire Pauline scheme of salvation by Grace is tinged with Gnostic hues and betrays the influence of Paul's upbringing on his theology. When we understand the general mechanics of Gnostic attitudes about God (theology), the world (cosmology), and Man (anthropology), then we can identify their parallels in Pauline Christology. "Paul's Epistles show a form of Gnosticism which is worth isolating, though it is combined with other, non-Gnostic mythological elements to which we shall come later." The main features of Gnosticism in Pauline Christology have been highlighted by a number of academics.

Gnosticism's typical theology is built on the heresy that the Creator of the universe is an evil demigod — not the true God, who is transcendent, disinterested, and uninvolved with the world. Paul made some modifications to this Gnostic heresy. As we observe the similarities and modifications, recall what has preceded of the Gnostic reading of Paul's epistles and how they justified their beliefs with his teachings.

---

[193] Pagels, Elaine. The Gnostic Paul: Gnostic Exegesis of the Pauline Letters, pp. 158-159.

> In Gnosticism, this world is regarded as so evil that it cannot have been created by God... The basic perception of Gnosticism is certainly present in Paul: that this world is so sunk in evil that rescue from above is a necessity. But the mythological details are modified. Paul does not think that the world was actually created by an evil power; he accepts the account of Genesis that the world was created by God. But he believes that the world has come under the control and lordship of an evil power; the Earth is captured territory. This is why there can be no hope of salvation except from outside.
>
> The importance of the concept of an evil power or the Devil in Paul's thought, or rather mythology, cannot be overestimated. When referring to this power or powers, he generally uses expressions derived from Gnosticism rather than from Judaism. Thus, he gives a picture of the assault of cosmic evil powers on Jesus in these words: 'None of this world's rulers knew this wisdom; for if they had known it, they would not have crucified the glorious Lord' (i Corinthians 2: 8). The expression 'this world's rulers' (*archonton tou aionos toutou*) does not refer to earthly rulers such as the Romans or the High Priest, but to supernatural powers who rule over 'this world' in the sense of 'this cosmic era'. Similarly, he uses the expression 'principalities and powers' and other such expressions with Gnostic connections to refer to the supernatural forces that oppose Jesus and himself (e.g. Romans 8:38). On one occasion, he even calls the supreme evil force a 'god' (II Corinthians 4: 4).[194]

As is highlighted above, the cosmology and world-view that is typical of Gnosticism states that the physical world is an evil place — a dark prison which must be escaped. We have seen how Paul portrayed the world as under the control of evil supernatural forces, a decidedly pessimistic outlook that is common to deviant belief systems.

---

194 Maccoby. The Mythmaker. p. 186.

> Recent discoveries have shown that, contrary to what was previously argued, Gnosticism existed before Christianity, though it later took Christian forms... Paul thus thinks of the forces of evil as organized in a hierarchy and as having power independent of God, at least for a period in cosmic history. It was primarily to break the power of these forces that Jesus came to the world; though the earthly power that opposed him, that of the Jews, seemed to be his main enemies, this was only on the surface, for he was engaged, in reality, in a vast cosmic struggle in which his earthly antagonists were the pawns of evil supernatural forces.[195]

Gnostic 'anthropology' generally states that Man is a prisoner in an evil world and can only achieve salvation from this prison by means of inner-enlightenment, upon which the enlightened human becomes one with the Godhead.

> The essence of the Gnostic myth was that this world is in the grip of evil, and that therefore a visitor (or a series of visitors) is necessary from the world of Light, in order to impart the secret knowledge (gnosis) by which some privileged souls may escape from the thrall of this world...What imprisons us is the human condition, which is one of bondage to the powers of Evil. From this aspect of the story comes what theologians call the doctrine of Original Sin, a re-reading by Paul of the Hebrew story about the ejection of Adam and Eve from the Garden of Eden, which in the story itself, and its traditional Jewish exegesis, did not have this radical connotation. So far the story is the same as that found in the type of religion known as Gnosticism.[196]

We have seen how the convergence of philosophy and gnostic mysticism played a pivotal role in forever altering the scriptural record and the development of Church doctrine. The mystical

---

195 ibid.

196 ibid.

gnostic approach of inner-enlightenment that transformed the early church survives until today where mainstream Christians imagine themselves to be inwardly directed by the 'holy spirit' to interpret scripture according to their personal whims and preferences. This has resulted in the endless fragmenting of Christian denominations, each of them following their intuitions and inspirations, proving utterly gullible and susceptible to the machinations of devils.

The Pauline Impact on Western Thought

Understanding the development of Western thought from its ancient pagan roots until the Christianization of Europe, or instead, we should say the paganization of Christianity, is vital to understanding the contemporary Western mind. As we have seen, the syncretic blend of the pagan mysteries of Egypt and Mesopotamia were then rationalized and repurposed by the Greek Philosophers. In the same way, the mystery pagan religions and Greek philosophy would fuse with Judaism and then Christianity and change it forever. It is essential to identify the corruptive influence of encapsulating cultures, precisely that of the Greco-Roman and Persian variety. Both Greek philosophy and mystical, mystery religions, such as Iranian dualistic Zoroastrianism, had unmistakable formative effects on early Christians. Not surprisingly, the traces of the pessimistic Gnostic world-view are still a permanent feature of Western thought:

> Western culture is based on the twin pillars of Greek rationality, on the one hand, and biblical faith, on the other...However, from the first centuries to the present day there has also existed a third current, characterized by a resistance to the dominance of either pure rationality or doctrinal faith. The adherents of

this tradition emphasized the importance of inner-enlightenment or gnosis.[197]

As we have seen, these three sources of Western culture date back to the earliest times and have played a never-ending role in altering revealed religion. Professor Carroll Quigley touts what he sees to be the crowning achievement of this dizzying syncretic blending of creeds that has produced modern Western thought. He says:

> Western religious thought has continued to believe that **revelation itself is never final, total, complete, or literal, but is a continuous symbolic process that must be interpreted and reinterpreted by discussion**. The method of the West, even in religion, has been this: The truth unfolds in time by a cooperative process of discussion that creates a temporary consensus which we hope will form successive approximations growing closer and closer to the final truth, to be reached only in some final stage of eternity.
>
> In the Christian tradition the stages in this unfolding process for each individual are numerous; they include: (1) man's intuitive sense of natural law and morality, (2) the Old Testament, (3) the New Testament, (4) the long series of Church councils and ecclesiastical promulgations that will continue indefinitely into the future, (5) for each individual a continued process of knowledge in eternity after death, and, finally, (6) the Beatific Vision. Until this final stage, **all versions of the truth, even when their factual content is based on divine revelation, must be understood and interpreted by community discussion in terms of past experiences and traditions**...

[197] van den Broek, R., & Hanegraaff, W. J. (Eds.). (1998). Gnosis and hermeticism from Antiquity to modern times. SUNY (State University of NY) Press. p. vii

...These procedures that I have identified as Western, and have illustrated from the rather unpromising field of religion, are to be found in all aspects of Western life.[198]

In another popular work, he further explains this syncretic outlook at the foundation of Western thought. He identifies this as the lens to understand all of Western history, saying:

> This attitude...**the social unfolding of the truth, is the basis of the Western religious outlook**. This outlook believed that religious truth unfolded in time and is not yet complete. The Old Testament, for example, was not canceled or replaced by the New Testament but was supplemented by it.
>
> And **the New Testament was never, in most of the life of Western civilization, regarded as a literal, explicit, and final statement of the truth.** Rather, recognition of its truths have to be developed in time, by social action, from basically symbolic statements. Thus the doctrine of the Christian church was unfolded through church councils (like that at Nicaea) and by conferences of learned doctors and clerics, without ever any feeling that the process was finished.
>
> The fundamentalist position on biblical interpretation, with its emphasis on the explicit, complete, final, and authoritarian nature of Scripture, is a very late, minority view quite out of step with the Western tradition.[199]

What Quigley described above is a useful guideline for understanding the syncretic nature of Christian, and thus Western thought: a perpetual process of the unfolding of truth and the bending and relativity of morality according to the whims and caprice of the religious and political elite. Were one to be mindful of the heavy syncretic pagan influences on every source of influence on Western thought as mentioned above, then that

---

[198] Quigley. Tragedy and Hope, pp. 1229-1231.

[199] Quigley. The Evolution of Civilizations, pp. 341-342.

will lay bare for the objective observer the West's expectations pertaining reformation in general. Thus he would better understand their expectations of reform for Islam and the Muslim world.

Chapter Conclusion

As we have seen in this chapter, the culmination of these compounded factors proved to overwhelm the earliest community until, ultimately, subverting and supplanting the original teachings of Jesus (عَلَيْهِ ٱلسَّلَامُ), effectively paganizing Christianity ever since. Consider the core concept at the heart of the doctrine of the Trinity: a transcendent 'God' in heaven, an earthly 'god' in the physical form of flesh and blood, and a spiritual 'god' residing within and directing the practitioners of the faith, who by mystic ritual and sacraments aim to attain oneness with the Divine. In this scheme, both Prophet and community are, by extension, assigned a portion of Divinity. This alone is sufficient to demonstrate Christianity's total paganization. Now, add to that an insidious, hidden undercurrent of subversive Gnostic elites claiming to have special inner-knowledge, enlightenment, and hidden scriptures. These 'Gnostics' had a mixed origin traceable to early Jewish apocalypticism and the Middle Platonism of the mystic, Philo of Alexandria, a Hellenized Jew who viewed scripture as allegorical. Beyond that, the elitist Gnostics ideology is traceable to Eastern mystery religions, specifically to Iranian dualistic Zoroastrianism. Recall how they infiltrated the Church early on to incrementally change it from within. Add to all of that the primitive, pagan hoards of Europe and Asia Minor that were Christianized over the course of subsequent generations, rewording and repurposing their ancient native rituals and beliefs to carry a Christian label forevermore. By the early fourth century, paganism was officially

Christianized, and Christianity was forever paganized. This alone is sufficient reason to demonstrate the inevitable necessity for the advent of Islam shortly after that.

Imagine the indiscernibility of any purported 'orthodox' Christianity to the isolated, illiterate, superstitious masses of Europe and imagine their susceptibility to succumb to superstition and exploitation of every sort and at every opportunity. To what degree can Christian teachings retain any meaningful claim to orthodoxy and authenticity? More importantly, to what degree has the default essence of Western culture been defined by this gnostic 'inner-enlightenment' and quest for the apotheosis and divination of man that defines Christian doctrine? These questions may perturb a practicing Christian and offend their sensibilities, yet when Muslim history receives the same inquiry as to its origins and gradual alterations, it is seemingly fair game to the Western mind. On the other hand, any objective, knowledgeable Muslim would readily concede the historical impact of both Western philosophy and Eastern esotericism on the beliefs of many or even most Muslims as being an undeniable reality; yet the primary sources and original teachings of Islam have remained miraculously intact against all odds — not so for the sources of Christianity.

Part III: the Encroachment of Deviant Belief Systems & the Decline of Muslim Civilization

Chapter Five: The Swift Triumph of the Sunnah & The Gradual Encroachment of Foreign Creeds

The Advent of Islam & Its Rapid Spread

Shaykh al Islām Ibn Taymiyyah (رَحِمَهُ ٱللَّهُ) outlines the signs and proofs of the prophethood and Messengership of Muḥammad (صَلَّى ٱللَّهُ عَلَيْهِ وَسَلَّمَ):[200]

> The biography of the Messenger (صَلَّى ٱللَّهُ عَلَيْهِ وَسَلَّمَ), as well as his character, statements, actions, and revealed law are from his signs. The knowledge of his nation and their religiosity are also from his evidence. The miracles graced upon the righteous of his Ummah are likewise from his signs. That becomes manifest upon reflection over his biography, from his birth to his advent, and then from his emergence until his death; likewise is the case with reflecting upon his lineage, homeland, his origins and what he produced.

{The Legacy of Abraham}

> For assuredly, he was from the noblest household in stock, from the core of the bloodline of Abraham, in whose progeny Allah (تَبَارَكَ وَتَعَالَىٰ) placed the prophethood and scripture. No prophet came after Abraham (عَلَيْهِ ٱلسَّلَامُ) except from his progeny. He gave him two sons: Ishmael and Isaac (عَلَيْهِمَا ٱلسَّلَامُ). Both are mentioned in the Torah. Glad tidings about what would become of the children of Ishmael are provided in the Torah. No-one from Ishmael's children appeared with what the prophecies foretold besides him. Abraham (عَلَيْهِ ٱلسَّلَامُ) supplicated Allah for Ishmael's progeny, asking that He dispatch a Messenger amongst them from themselves. Furthermore, he

200 Ibn Taymiyyah. Al Jawāb al-Ṣaḥīḥ li man baddala Dīn al Masīḥ v.5, p. 437.

was from Quraish, the elect of Abraham's tribe; beyond that, he was from the Tribe of Hāshim, the elect of Quraish; still yet, he was from Mecca, the mother of towns and the homeland of the House (of worship) built by Abraham (عَلَيْهِ السَّلَام), and to which he summoned the people to make pilgrimage. It did not cease being visited in pilgrimage since the era of Abraham and was mentioned with the most attractive description in the scriptures of the prophets.

{His Upbringing and Noble Character}

He (عَلَيْهِ الصَّلَاةُ وَالسَّلَام) was the most complete of people in (his) upbringing and raising. He was always known for truthfulness, reverence, justice, noble character, and for abstaining from licentiousness, oppression, and every contemptuous trait. This fact was attested to for him by all who knew him before the prophethood: by those who believed in him and by those who disbelieved in him. They knew nothing morally damaging about him. There was nothing of the sort found in his statements, actions or character. Never once was he perceived to be lying, oppressing, or being licentious. His appearance and countenance were the most perfect and inclusive of handsome features, demonstrative of his perfection. He was unlettered, from illiterate people, to whom the people of Torah and Evangelical scriptures were alien, just as his people were alien to them. He had never read anything of Man's knowledge, nor had he held an audience with their learned ones. He did not claim prophethood until Allah (تَبَارَكَ وَتَعَالَى) had completed forty years of his life. After this, he procured a matter most astonishing and magnificent: words whose equivalence the earlier and later generations had never heard. He informed us of a significant affair to which none in his homeland and people had known anything compatible.

{How He Attracted Followers}

After this, the followers of the Prophets — the weak and the vulnerable — followed him, whereas the people of leadership belied him and showed him enmity. They strove in every way for his and his followers' destruction — just as the unbelievers had previously done with the Prophets and their followers. Those who followed him did not do so out of incentive or terror, for indeed he had not any wealth to bestow upon them, nor any positions to appoint to them. He did not have the sword with him, but rather the sword, wealth and status were on the side of his enemies. They abused his followers with a variety of abuses, but they remained patient, seeking divine reward, not apostatizing from their religion due to the sweetness of faith and knowledge that had merged with their hearts.

The Arabs had been making Ḥajj (pilgrimage to Mecca) since the time of Abraham (عَلَيْهِ السَّلَام), so the Arab tribes would congregate during the season (of Ḥajj), upon which he would come out to them, conveying the message and inviting them to Allah, being patient in what encountered of belying, mistreatment, and the disinterestedness from people. Ultimately he held assembled with the people of Yathrib, who had been neighbors with the Jews, having heard reports about him from them, due to which they recognized him. Once he invited them (to Islam), they knew that he was the awaited prophet about whom the Jews had foretold. They had already heard portents of his advent by which they recognized his status. For assuredly, his affair had become wide-known and preeminent over the course of ten-odd years. So they believed in him, and they pledged an oath of allegiance for he and his companions to migrate to their land, and that they would strive alongside him. So he and those who followed him migrated to al Madīnah, which was thenceforth inhabited by the Muhājirūn (those who fled persecution) and the Anṣār (the Supporters).

None of them had believed for worldly incentive or out of fear, to the exception of a few amongst the Anṣār who outwardly accepted Islam, some of whom later beautifully practiced Islam. Subsequently, permission for Jihād (struggle) was given to him, then he was commanded with it.

He never ceased establishing Allah's commandment wholly and correctly, instituting truthfulness, justice, and integrity. Not a single lie or act of oppression or treachery was recorded against him. Instead, he proved to be most honest and fair, and was the most loyal to his covenant, despite the assortment of scenarios that he faced, consisting of war and peace, safety and fear, wealth and impoverishment, scarcity and abundance, sometimes being preeminent over his adversary, and sometimes the enemy being dominant over him.

Throughout all of that, he abided by the most perfect and complete of mannerisms, until the invitation ultimately became preeminent in all of the lands of the Arabs which had priorly been replete with idolatry, fortune-telling, obedience to the creation in disbelief of the Most Merciful, the shedding of inviolable blood, and severance of ties of kinship. They had been unfamiliar with a hereafter or resurrection (for Judgment). Then they became the most knowledgeable, most religious, fairest, and virtuous people on earth, to such an extent that when the Christians saw them when they arrived in the Levant, they exclaimed: those who accompanied the Messiah were not more virtuous than these. The impact of their knowledge and deeds are evident in the earth in comparison to the influences of others. Intelligent people can recognize the difference between the two matters.

Despite the preeminence of his affair and peoples' obedience to him, and their assigning him primacy over their own lives and property, he died without leaving behind so much as a *dīnār* or *dirhām*, not even owning a sheep or beast of burden. All he had was his mule and weapon, and his armor, which was being held as collateral with a Jew for thirty Ṣā' of barley that he purchased for his family. He owned properties from which he used to spend upon his family while using the rest of the proceeds for the needs of the Muslims. He issued a judgment that he would not leave it as inheritance, nor would his inheritors take anything from it.

For the duration of this time, astonishing signs and an assortment of miracles perpetually appeared at his hands, whose description requires exhaustive length. He foretold for them the news of what was yet to come. He ordered them with goodness and forbade them from evil, declared all that is wholesome to be permitted while prohibiting all that was impure. He legislated the laws, one after another, until Allah تَبَارَكَ وَتَعَالَى ultimately completed His religion by him. Nothing recognized as goodness by the sound intellects remained except that he ordered with it. Nothing realized by sound intellects to be evil remained except that he forbade it. He never ordered something about which it would be said, if only he had not commanded that; and he never forbade anything about which it would be said if only he had not prohibited it. He permitted all wholesome things, not prohibiting anything of the sort in the way that they had been in the religious laws of others. He banned impurities, not allowing any of them, as others had sanctioned.

He assembled within himself all of the attractive qualities which the nations had long incorporated. The Torah, Evangels, or Psalms have mentioned nothing about Allah, His Angels, or about the Last Day except that he perfectly came with the same and even informed of matters not found in other scriptures. There is no obliging of justice, graciousness in arbitration, encouragement of virtues, or incentive to righteousness, except that he came with what was like it or better. When an intelligent person looks at the acts of worship he legislated in comparison to those of other nations, then its superiority and predominance will be apparent; the same is the case with punishments and rulings, and the remainder of revealed matters of religion.

The Prophet's Virtuous Nation was His Legacy

His nation is the most complete regarding all virtue. Were their knowledge to be contrasted to that of the remaining nations, then the superiority of their knowledge would be apparent. If their religiosity, worship, and obedience to Allah were compared to that of others, then it would also be evident that they are more religious than others. Were their courage, their striving in Allah's path, and their patience over hardships for Allah's sake to be comparatively measured, then it would be apparent that they are greater in striving and are more brave-hearted. If their generosity, sacrificing, and good-naturedness was compared to that of others, it would become clear that they are more generous and honorable than others. They procured and learned these virtues from him. It is he who instructed them accordingly. They had not previously followed a scripture which he had come to complete, as the Messiah عَلَيْهِ ٱلصَّلَاةُ وَٱلسَّلَامُ had come to fulfill the law of the Torah. Elements of the virtues and knowledge of the Messiah's followers were extant within the Torah, portions were in the Psalms, and other elements were still within the annals of the prophets. Moreover, some of them were from the Messiah and others came from those after him, such as the apostles. They (i.e., the Christians) had even utilized the speech of the philosophers and others, to such an extent that upon altering his religion, they included many of affairs of the unbelievers that contradicted the Messiah's faith with Christ's religion.

As for the nation of Muḥammad صَلَّى ٱللَّٰهُ عَلَيْهِ وَسَلَّمَ, then they had not previously read a scripture. Instead, most of them had not believed in Moses, Jesus, David, the Torah, the Gospels, and the Psalms except through him. So it was he who ordered them to believe in all of the prophets and to concede the truth of the books revealed by Allah. He forbade them from discriminating pertaining belief in any of the prophets. (Allah) said in the book that he came (to us) with:

﴿قُولُوا آمَنَّا بِاللَّهِ وَمَا أُنْزِلَ إِلَيْنَا وَمَا أُنْزِلَ إِلَى إِبْرَاهِيمَ وَإِسْمَاعِيلَ وَإِسْحَاقَ وَيَعْقُوبَ وَالْأَسْبَاطِ وَمَا أُوتِيَ مُوسَى وَعِيسَى وَمَا أُوتِيَ النَّبِيُّونَ مِنْ رَبِّهِمْ لَا نُفَرِّقُ بَيْنَ أَحَدٍ مِنْهُمْ وَنَحْنُ لَهُ مُسْلِمُونَ. فَإِنْ آمَنُوا بِمِثْلِ مَا آمَنْتُمْ بِهِ فَقَدِ اهْتَدَوْا وَإِنْ تَوَلَّوْا فَإِنَّمَا هُمْ فِي شِقَاقٍ فَسَيَكْفِيكَهُمُ اللَّهُ وَهُوَ السَّمِيعُ الْعَلِيمُ﴾

"136. Say (O Muslims), "We believe in Allah and that which has been sent down to us and that which has been sent down to Ibrahim (Abraham), Ishmael, Isaac, Jacob, and to Al-Asbat [the twelve sons of Ya'qub (Jacob)], and that which has been given to Musa (Moses) and 'Iesa (Jesus), and that which has been given to the Prophets from their Lord. We make no distinction between any of them, and to Him we have submitted (in Islam). So if they believe in the like of that which you believe, then they are rightly guided, but if they turn away, then they are only in opposition. So Allah will suffice you against them. And He is the All-Hearer, the All-Knower."[201]

Also, He said:

﴿آمَنَ الرَّسُولُ بِمَا أُنْزِلَ إِلَيْهِ مِنْ رَبِّهِ وَالْمُؤْمِنُونَ كُلٌّ آمَنَ بِاللَّهِ وَمَلَائِكَتِهِ وَكُتُبِهِ وَرُسُلِهِ لَا نُفَرِّقُ بَيْنَ أَحَدٍ مِنْ رُسُلِهِ وَقَالُوا سَمِعْنَا وَأَطَعْنَا غُفْرَانَكَ رَبَّنَا وَإِلَيْكَ الْمَصِيرُ - لَا يُكَلِّفُ اللَّهُ نَفْسًا إِلَّا وُسْعَهَا لَهَا مَا كَسَبَتْ وَعَلَيْهَا مَا اكْتَسَبَتْ رَبَّنَا لَا تُؤَاخِذْنَا إِنْ نَسِينَا أَوْ أَخْطَأْنَا رَبَّنَا وَلَا تَحْمِلْ عَلَيْنَا إِصْرًا كَمَا حَمَلْتَهُ عَلَى الَّذِينَ مِنْ قَبْلِنَا رَبَّنَا وَلَا تُحَمِّلْنَا مَا لَا طَاقَةَ لَنَا بِهِ وَاعْفُ عَنَّا وَاغْفِرْ لَنَا وَارْحَمْنَا أَنْتَ مَوْلَانَا فَانْصُرْنَا عَلَى الْقَوْمِ الْكَافِرِينَ﴾

"285. The Messenger (Muhammad ﷺ) believes in what has been sent down to him from his Lord, and (so do) the believers. Each one believes in Allah, His Angels, His Books, and His Messengers. They say, "We make no distinction between one another of His Messengers" - and they say, "We hear, and we obey. (We seek) Your Forgiveness, our Lord, and to You is the return (of all). 286. Allah burdens not a person

[201] Al Baqarah: 136-137

beyond his scope. He gets reward for that (good) which he has earned, and he is punished for that (evil) which he has earned. "Our Lord! Punish us not if we forget or fall into error, our Lord! Lay not on us a burden like that which You did lay on those before us (Jews and Christians); our Lord! Put not on us a burden greater than we have strength to bear. Pardon us and grant us Forgiveness. Have mercy on us. You are our Maula (Patron, Supporter and Protector, etc.) and give us victory over the disbelieving people."[202]

The Intolerance of His Nation for Foreign Beliefs or Practices being Inserted into Islam

His nation does not permit taking something as a matter of religion from outside of what he brought. They do not innovate innovations for which Allah (تَبَارَكَ وَتَعَالَى) revealed no authority. So they do not legislate what Allah (تَبَارَكَ وَتَعَالَى) has not permitted of religion. Instead, they take lesson from that which he (صَلَّى ٱللَّهُ عَلَيْهِ وَسَلَّمَ) narrated about stories of the Prophets and their nations. As for what the People of the Book recount to them that agrees with what they already have, then they affirm it. They stop short from believing anything that they cannot discern truth from falsehood about. Whatever they recognize as falsehood they reject. Whoever inserts into their religion what does not belong to it — from the statements of the philosophers of India, Persia, Greece, and others — then they consider him to be from the adherents of deviation and aberration. This is the religion that the *Ṣaḥābah* of Allah's Messenger and their successors were upon. It is that which the Imams of the faith were upon, those who recognized as having tongues of veracity amongst the Ummah. It is that which the main-body and masses of Muslims are upon. Whoever departs from that is deemed contemptuous and misled in the view of the community. That is the way of the *Ahlus-Sunnah was*

---

202 Al Baqarah: 285-286.

Jamā'ah, who will remain preeminent upon the truth until the establishment of the Hour — those about whom the Prophet (صَلَّىٰ ٱللَّٰهُ عَلَيْهِ وَسَلَّمَ) said:

لَا تَزَالُ طَائِفَةٌ مِنْ أُمَّتِي ظَاهِرِينَ عَلَى الْحَقِّ، لَا يَضُرُّهُمْ مَنْ خَالَفَهُمْ وَلَا مَنْ خَذَلَهُمْ، حَتَّى تَقُومَ السَّاعَةُ

"There shall never cease to be a faction of my nation who are victorious upon the truth; they shall not be harmed by those who oppose them, nor those who forsake them, until the Hour is established."

Perhaps some Muslims may differ, while still agreeing upon this foundation, which constitutes the religion of the Messengers (عَلَيْهِمُ ٱلسَّلَامُ) in general, and that of Muḥammad in specific. However, whoever differs regarding this foundation is a detested *mulḥid* (heretic), contrary to the case of the Christians who innovated another religion that was instituted by their senior scholars and ascetics and was fought over by their kings, only to be ritually practiced by their masses despite it being an innovated religion

Allah تَبَارَكَ وَتَعَالَىٰ sent his Messengers with beneficial knowledge and righteous action. So whoever follows the Messengers (عَلَيْهِمُ ٱلسَّلَامُ) attains felicity in this world and in the Hereafter. **Those who enter into (religious) innovation are only those who fall short of following the Prophets in knowledge and action.** So once Allah (تَبَارَكَ وَتَعَالَىٰ) sent Muḥammad with guidance and the religion of truth, the Muslims, his nation, received that from him; so all beneficial knowledge and righteous action that his nation is upon, they took directly from their Prophet (صَلَّىٰ ٱللَّٰهُ عَلَيْهِ وَسَلَّمَ). Along with this, it is obvious to every person that his nation is the most complete in all virtues pertinent to knowledge and implementation. It is known that every perfection found in the student branches off from the original teacher, necessitating that he was the most perfect person in knowledge and religiosity (صَلَّىٰ ٱللَّٰهُ عَلَيْهِ وَسَلَّمَ). These matters necessitate that one has certain knowledge that he was truthful in saying:

﴿إِنِّي رَسُولُ اللَّهِ إِلَيْكُمْ جَمِيعًا﴾

"I am Allah's Messenger to you all."[203]...[204]

Al Maqrīzī (رَحِمَهُ ٱللَّهُ) (died 845 h.) summarized the attractive simplicity of Islam in its pristine form in its earliest generation. He says:

> Know that when Allah (تَبَارَكَ وَتَعَالَىٰ) sent His Prophet Muhammad (صَلَّى ٱللَّهُ عَلَيْهِ وَسَلَّمَ) from the Arabs as a Messenger to all people, he described their Lord to them as He had described Himself in His noble book and just as He had revealed upon his heart by medium of the Ruḥ al Amīn (the Trustworthy Spirit, i.e. Jibrīl عَلَيْهِ ٱلصَّلَاةُ وَٱلسَّلَامُ) — just as Allah (تَبَارَكَ وَتَعَالَىٰ) had revealed to him. Not a single one of the Arabs in their entirety, whether from the townsfolk or the Bedouins, asked him about the meaning of any of that, as they used to ask him about the commandments pertaining prayer, alms-giving, fasting, pilgrimage, and things besides that which Allah had ordered or forbidden. Nor did they do so as they used to ask him about the circumstances of Judgment Day, Paradise, and Hellfire. If one of them had asked him about the Divine Attributes, then this would have been reported. As were narrations regarding the rulings of ḥalāl and ḥarām (the lawful and unlawful), *targhīb* and *tarhīb* (encouragement and discouragement), the events of Judgement Day, the major battles and the tribulation (in the last days), and whatever is similar to that, as is contained in the books of ḥadīth — in the *Ma'ājim*, *Masānīd*, and *Jawāmi'*.[205]

---

[203] Al 'Arāf: 158

[204] Ibn Taymiyyah. Al Jawāb al-Ṣaḥīḥ, Vol. 5, pp. 437-445.

[205] various collections of ḥadīth written with different styles.

> Whoever investigates the annals of *ḥadīth* and comes across the reports of the salaf will know that there is no chain of transmission, whether authentic or inauthentic, reporting that any one of the Ṣaḥāba — despite their multiple generations and multitudes — ever asked Allah's Messenger (صَلَّى ٱللَّهُ عَلَيْهِ وَسَلَّمَ) about the meaning of anything in the Quran of what Allah (تَبَارَكَ وَتَعَالَىٰ) described about Himself or anything as such from the tongue of His Prophet Muhammad (صَلَّى ٱللَّهُ عَلَيْهِ وَسَلَّمَ). Rather, all of them understood what that meant and were silent about speculative rhetoric regarding the Divine Attributes. Yes, and likewise, they did not discriminate between whether it was an Attribute of Essence or an attribute of action. They simply affirmed His Eternal Attributes such as Omniscience (boundless knowledge), Omnipotence (boundless power), Eternality, Divine Will, Hearing, Seeing, Speech, Majesty and Honoring, Generosity and Blessing, Might, and Magnificence. They conveyed the speech in a single fashion, and in the same way they absolutely described Him as having a Face, Hands and the likes, while negating His having any resemblance to the creation. **None of them endeavored to further interpret any of it.** They all saw it fit to leave the Attributes just as they had been conveyed. None of them had something special by which they tried to prove Allah's Oneness and the Prophethood of Muhammad (صَلَّى ٱللَّهُ عَلَيْهِ وَسَلَّمَ), except for Allah's Book. **None of them were familiar with anything of the methods of speculative theology or the issues of philosophy.**[206]

As Al Maqrīzī (رَحِمَهُ ٱللَّهُ) has clearly alluded to in the above passage, it was, in fact, the simplicity of Islamic teachings that originally carried the greatest appeal for the masses. The French academic Edouard Montet (1856-1934 CE) stated:

> A creed so precise, so stripped of all theological complexities and consequently so accessible to the ordinary understanding, might be expected to possess and does indeed possess a

[206] Al Mawā'iẓ wal I'tibār, vol. 4, p. 188.

> marvelous power of winning its way into the consciousness of men.[207]

History proves that the earliest Muslim scholars were most diligent in retaining doctrinal purity and combatting these foreign influences, methodically refuting them with authentic, explicit religious texts. Despite that, within the first few centuries, many significant fundamental deviations in theology and practice became mainstream in the Muslim world. Montet observed as much when he noted:

> The simplicity and the clearness of this teaching are certainly among the most obvious forces at work in the religion and the missionary activity of Islam. It cannot be denied that many doctrines and systems of theology and also many superstitions, from the worship of saints to the use of rosaries and amulets, have become grafted on to the main trunk of the Muslim creed.[208]

Likewise, Al Maqrīzī (رَحِمَهُ ٱللَّهُ) very accurately summarizes the foreign source of the eventual convolution and complication of Islam's doctrinal simplicity:

> The root of all innovation in the religion is being distant from the speech of the Salaf and deviating from the creed of the first generation.... The domain of imagination is vast and preeminent rule belongs to delusion. So the minds conflicted and the fallacies grew ample, at which point each party went to great lengths in evil, stubbornness, transgression, and corruption to the furthest extent and most distant extremity. They mutually hated and cursed each other, deeming both the property and lives of others as violable. They triumphed only by the help of

[207] Arnold, Thomas Walker. The preaching of Islam, p. 307.

[208] ibid.

states and they sought the aid of kings... And they will never cease differing, except for those your Lord spares.[209]

The Beginning of the Tribulation

In documenting the proliferation and popularization of deviant doctrines, I have focused mainly on three different passages found (1.) in the history of Al Maqrīzī, (2.) in Ibn al Qayyim's *Ṣawā'iq al Mursalah*, and (3.) in Majmū' al Fatāwā, the popular collection of Ibn Taymiyyah's writings.

Towards the end of his well known history book al Mawā'iẓ wal I'tibār, Al Maqrīzī (رحمه الله) summarizes many centuries of doctrinal schisms eventuating in the crisis of the decline of Muslim civilization:

> This — may Allah honor you — is an explanation of the creeds of the Ummah from the beginning of the affair until this time of ours. I have explained in detail what historians have summarized, while summarizing what they explained in detail. You — oh student of knowledge — merely have to accept what I have toiled in of labor and have worked on extensively, turning the pages through the annals of Islam and the books of history. It has reached you in pristine form, and you have taken it for free, without any burden of difficulty or having sacrificed any effort...[210]

Shaykh al Islām Aḥmad b. 'Abd al Ḥamīd b. Taymiyyah al Ḥarrānī (رحمه الله) (died 728 h.) explains the gradual weakening if the branches and roots of faith in detail. He explains:

---

209 Al Maqrīzī. Al Mawā'iẓ wal I'tibār, Vol. 4, p. 198.

210 Al Mawā'iẓ wal I'tibār, vol. 4, p. 193.

Know that most innovations related to matters of knowledge and worship... only began during the end of the era of the rightly guided caliphs, just as the Prophet (ﷺ) foretold. He said:

مَنْ يَعِشْ مِنْكُمْ بَعْدِي فَسَيَرَى اخْتِلَافًا كَثِيرًا ، فَعَلَيْكُمْ بِسُنَّتِي وَسُنَّةِ الْخُلَفَاءِ الرَّاشِدِينَ الْمَهْدِيِّينَ مِنْ بَعْدِي

"Whoever of you lives after me will see great differing, so it is upon you to abide by my Sunnah and the Sunnah of the rightly guided caliphs after me."

It is known that when those charged with authority — those who arbitrate pertaining people's lives and property — are upright, then the masses of people will be upright. This is just as Abu Bakr Al-Ṣiddīq (رضي الله عنه) stated — as Bukhārī (رحمه الله) narrates in his *Ṣaḥīḥ* — that when the Aḥmasiyyah woman asked, "How long shall we remain upon this state of rectitude?" He said, "So long as your Imāms remain upright for you." One narration says, "There are two groups who, so long as they are righteous, then the people will be righteous: the scholars and the rulers." They are the people of scripture and the people of iron as is demonstrated by (Allah's) statement:

﴿ لَقَدْ أَرْسَلْنَا رُسُلَنَا بِالْبَيِّنَاتِ وَأَنزَلْنَا مَعَهُمُ الْكِتَابَ وَالْمِيزَانَ لِيَقُومَ النَّاسُ بِالْقِسْطِ ۖ وَأَنزَلْنَا الْحَدِيدَ فِيهِ بَأْسٌ شَدِيدٌ وَمَنَافِعُ لِلنَّاسِ وَلِيَعْلَمَ اللَّهُ مَن يَنصُرُهُ وَرُسُلَهُ بِالْغَيْبِ ۚ إِنَّ اللَّهَ قَوِيٌّ عَزِيزٌ ﴾

"Indeed We have sent Our Messengers with clear proofs, and revealed with them the Scripture and the Balance (justice) that mankind may keep up justice. And We brought forth iron wherein is mighty power (in matters of war), as well as many benefits for mankind, that Allah may test who it is that will help Him (His religion), and His Messengers in the unseen. Verily, Allah is All-Strong, All-Mighty."[211]

They are the people of command meant by (Allah's) statement:

[211] Al Ḥadīd: 25.

﴿ يَا أَيُّهَا الَّذِينَ آمَنُوا أَطِيعُوا اللَّهَ وَأَطِيعُوا الرَّسُولَ وَأُولِي الْأَمْرِ مِنكُمْ ﴾

"O you who believe! Obey Allah and obey the Messenger (Muhammad ﷺ), and those of you (Muslims) who are in authority."[212]

Likewise, through them corruption occurs, just as has come in the narration from a number of the Ṣaḥāba: "What I fear most for you is the slip of the scholar, the hypocrite's use of the Qurān for disputation and the misguiding leaders."[213] The misguiding leaders are the rulers. Both the scholar and the disputer are knowledgeable people. However, the first has a sound creed yet errs, as happened with leaders of the *Fuqahā'* from *Ahl al-Sunnah wal Jamā'ah*; the second are those such as the philosophers and speculative theologians who use ambiguous doubts concerning the Quran for disputation, although, they have really forsaken the Quran. They only actually use it as an argument to overtake their opponent, instead of using it for guidance and relying upon it. For this reason, he (ﷺ) said "The hypocrites' disputation with the Qurān." For indeed the Quran, the Sunnah and the scholarly consensus refute his doubts.

The religion residing in the heart — comprising of faith as both knowledge and condition (*'ilm wa ḥāl*) — is the foundation. The external actions are the branches, which are the completion of faith. So the religion, firstly, is built from foundational roots and is (then) completed by its branches. This is similar to how Allah, in Makkah, revealed the roots of faith including tawḥīd, the parables — which are rational analogies, the stories (of the Prophets), divine promise (of reward), and divine threat (of punishment). Then, once he (the Prophet ﷺ) had power in al Madīnah, He (عَزَّوَجَلَّ) revealed its external branches such as

---

[212] Al-Nisā': 59.

[213] Collected by Al-Dārimī in his Sunan (220) and Ibn 'Abd al Barr in al Jāmi' (1867) authentically in mawqūf form, as the statement of 'Umar b. Al Khaṭṭāb.

al-Jumu'ah, the congregational prayers, the Adhān and Iqāma, Jihād, fasting, and the forbiddance of alcohol, fornication, gambling, and other things from its obligations and prohibitions. **So its roots supplement and reinforce its branches, while its branches complete and protect its roots. When obvious deficiency happens it initially does so through its branches.** For this reason, the Prophet (ﷺ) said, "The first thing you will lose of your religion is trustworthiness and the last thing you of your religion you will lose is the prayer." It was also reported from him that he said: The first thing taken will be judging with trustworthiness. Judging is the action of the rulers and those charged with authority, just as Allah said:

﴿إِنَّ اللَّهَ يَأْمُرُكُمْ أَنْ تُؤَدُّوا الْأَمَانَاتِ إِلَى أَهْلِهَا وَإِذَا حَكَمْتُمْ بَيْنَ النَّاسِ أَنْ تَحْكُمُوا بِالْعَدْلِ﴾

"Verily! Allah commands that you should render back the trusts to those, to whom they are due; and that when you judge between men, you judge with justice."[214]

As for the prayer, then it is the first obligation and is from the fundamentals of the religion and faith, joined alongside the testimony of faith, and as such will not depart except lastly. This is as the Prophet (ﷺ) said:

بدأ الإسلام غريباً وسيعود غريباً كما بدأ فطوبى للغرباء

"Islam began as something strange and will return to being something strange, so glad tidings of all good are for the strangers."

So he informed that it will return to how it was in the beginning.

Once the rule of the rightly guided Caliphs (رضي الله عنهم) departed, thereafter becoming a monarchy, then deficiency appeared amongst the rulers. So that also appeared, in turn, among the people of knowledge and religiosity. So in the end of the caliphate of 'Ali (رضي الله عنه), the innovations of the *Khawārij* and the

---

[214] Al-Nisā': 58

Rāfiḍah appeared, in as much as that they were related to leadership and the caliphate and other connected matters from the practices and rulings of the religion. The kingship of Mu'awiyyah (رَضِيَ ٱللَّهُ عَنْهُ) was a kingship and a mercy. Once Mu'awiyyah departed and the rule of Yazīd transpired, then the calamity of al-Ḥussayn's (رَضِيَ ٱللَّهُ عَنْهُ) murder happened in 'Irāq. Likewise, the civil strife of Al-Ḥarrah then happened in al-Madīnah, and they laid siege to Mecca when 'Abd Allah b. al-Zubayr (رَضِيَ ٱللَّهُ عَنْهُمَا) arose.

Then Yazīd died and the Ummah divided between Ibn Al-Zubayr (رَضِيَ ٱللَّهُ عَنْهُ) in the Ḥijāz and Banū'l Ḥakam in al-Shām. Al Mukhtār b. Abī 'Ubayd and others seized the opportunity in Iraq. That was at the end of the era of the Ṣaḥāba, amongst whom their remained: 'Abd Allah b. 'Abbās; Ibn 'Umar, Jābir b. 'Abd Allah, Abū Sa'īd al Khudrī and others (رَضِيَ ٱللَّهُ عَنْهُمْ).[215]

[Al Qadariyyah]

Al Maqrizī (رَحِمَهُ ٱللَّهُ) continues:

The Era of the Ṣaḥāba passed in this state, up until the doctrine about *al-qadar* (i.e. denial of predestiny) started. Meaning: the assertion that things just happen and that Allah did not preordain anything that the creation encounters. The first to speak about *al-qadar* in Islam was Ma'bad b. Khālid al Juhanī. He used to sit in the company of al Ḥasan b. Al Ḥussayn al Baṣrī (رَحِمَهُ ٱللَّهُ). It was he who spoke about *al qadar* in Baṣrah. His way destroyed the people of Baṣrah once they saw 'Amr b. 'Ubayd adopting it. This person Ma'bad had taken this opinion from a

---

215 Ibn Taymiyyah. Majmū' al Fatawā vol. 10, pp. 353-357.

man from the Asāwirah[216] called Abu Yunus Sansuweh, known as Al Uswārī.[217]

After causing substantial strife, he[218] was seized by Al Ḥajjāj, who crucified him in the year 80 h. at the order of 'Abdul Malik b. Marwān. When the doctrine of Ma'bad pertaining *al-qadar* reached 'Abd Allah b. 'Umar b. Al Khaṭṭāb (رَضِيَ اللَّهُ عَنْهُمَا), then he declared his innocence of him. A group of people followed Ma'bad in this innovation of his and so the Salaf took to dispraising the *Qadariyyah* and warning against them, as is well known in the books of ḥadīth.

'Aṭā b. Yassār was a judge who also held the view about *al qadar*. He and Ma'bad al Juhanī would go to Al Ḥasan al Baṣrī and say to him: These people are shedding blood and saying that our actions happen by Allah's predestining. So he (i.e., al Ḥasan رَحِمَهُ اللَّهُ) said: Allah's enemies have lied. So he was criticized for this and for what is similar to it.[219]

[Al Khawārij]

Ibn Taymiyyah (رَحِمَهُ اللَّهُ) writes:

---

[216] a family of Persian descent that took residence in Baṣrah and mingled with the Arab blood lines of Banu Tamīm. See Al Mu'allimī's foot notes in Al Ansāb of Al-Sama'ānī vol. 1, p. 258. Dar Ibn Taymiyyah (1400).

[217] see Al Qadar by Al Firyābī, narration 365. He was a person with no renown. His doctrine was spread by Ma'bad al Juhani and Ghaylān al-Dimashqi. Al Awzā'ī mentions that he was called Sawsan and that he was a Christian who become Muslim only to revert back to Christianity, after which Ma'bad adopted his practice and from him Ghaylān al-Dimashqī adopted it. See al-Sharī'ah by al Ajurī narration 555. Vol. 1, p. 959. Dār al Waṭn printing (1418).

[218] meaning Ma'bad al Juhanī.

[219] Al Mawā'iẓ wal i'tibār, pp. 188-189. Al Ḥasan al Baṣrī recanted his error pertaining al-qadar. He has many detailed statements advocating the correct belief in this issue. These statements have been gathered by Sh. Muqbil b. Hādī al Wādi'ī in his book Al Jāmi' al-Ṣaḥīḥ fi-l Qadar.

The more obvious innovations are in opposing the Messenger, the later they appear. The first to appear were only those which were less conspicuous in opposing the Book and the Sunnah, such as the innovation of the *Khawārij*. Despite that, authentic aḥādīth had come pertaining them, their dispraise, and their punishment; and the Ṣaḥābah were unanimous about that.[220]

Al Maqrizī (رَحِمَهُ ٱللَّهُ) continues:

Also, during the Era of the Ṣaḥābah (رَضِيَ ٱللَّهُ عَنْهُمْ), the doctrine of the *Khawārij* began. They explicitly pronounced excommunication for sin, and (called for) revolting and fighting of the ruler. So 'Abd Allah b. 'Abbās (رَضِيَ ٱللَّهُ عَنْهُمَا) debated them, yet they did not return to the truth. The Chief of the Believers, 'Ali b. Abī Ṭālib (رَضِيَ ٱللَّهُ عَنْهُ), fought them and killed a group of them — as is well known in the books of historical reports. A large number of people entered into the da'wah of the Khawārij and they accused a group of Islamic scholars of having entered into their way. A number of narrators of hadīth were counted amongst them as is known to those who specialize in that.[221]

[Al-Shi'ah Al-Rāfiḍah]

Al Maqrīzī (رَحِمَهُ ٱللَّهُ) continues:

Also, during the Era of the Ṣaḥāba, the doctrine of Shi'ism, (supposed allegiance) and fanaticism for 'Ali b. Abī Ṭālib (رَضِيَ ٱللَّهُ عَنْهُ) began. When that reached him, he disapproved of it and even burned a group of those with fanaticism. During his life, 'Abd Allah b. Wahb b. Saba', known popularly as Ibn al-Sawdā' Al-Saba'ī emerged. He introduced the doctrine of Allah's Messenger (صَلَّى ٱللَّهُ عَلَيْهِ وَسَلَّمَ) leaving a final will and testament

---

220 Al Ikhnā'iyyah. p. 213. Taḥqīq: Ahmed al 'Anzī. Dār al Khazār, Jeddah (1420/2000)

221 Al Mawā'iẓ wal i'tibār, p. 189.

commanding that the rulership must be for 'Ali, rendering him scripturally delegated to be the appointed successor after Allah's Messenger (صَلَّى ٱللَّٰهُ عَلَيْهِ وَسَلَّمَ). He also introduced the doctrine of Ali's return to the world after his death, as well as the return of Allah's Messenger. He claimed that Ali had not been killed — instead he remained alive and was partially divine — saying that he was ever-present in the clouds, the thunder being his voice and the lightning being his whip. So (according to his false claim) he must, by necessity, return back to the earth to fill it with justice, just as it was filled with oppression.

From this person, Ibn Saba', the different types of fanatical Rāfiḍah sprouted. They started professing the belief in al waqf, meaning that the rulership is an endowment restricted to certain specified people, such as the statement of the *Imāmiyyah* about the twelve Imams, and the statement of the *Ismā'iliyyah* that (rulership) was exclusively for the offspring of Ismā'īl b. Ja'far al-Ṣādiq. They also adopted from him the statement about the shadow of the Imam and his return to the world after death. It is similar to what the Imamiyyah believe pertaining the one who is to emerge from the crypt, which is, in fact, the belief in reincarnation. They also adopted from him statement a portion of divinity is incarnate in the Imams after Ali b. Abī Ṭālib, deeming them deserving of rulership by Divine mandate, similar to Adam deserving the angels' prostration. This view was a matter of creed for the proponents of Fatimid rule in Egypt.

It was this person, Ibn Saba', who instigated the strife against the Chief of the Believers 'Uthmān b. 'Affān, until he was ultimately killed, as Al Muqaffa mentioned in the biography of Ibn Saba' in al-Tārīkh al Kabīr. He had a number of acolytes and associates in most of the cities and provinces. By way of that, the Shi'ite became plentiful in number and became rivals of the Khawārij. Their affair did not cease strengthening and their numbers kept increasing.[222]

---

[222] Al Mawā'iẓ wal i'tibār, pp. 189-190.

Shaykh al Islām Ibn Taymiyyah (رَحِمَهُ ٱللَّهُ) said:

> At that point, they had not yet engaged in speculative theology about their Lord or His Attributes, and would not do so until the end of the *Umayyid* Dynasty, once most of the third generation — the successors to the tābi'īn — had departed. The three generations are counted according to when most of their generation are still present, which is the middle part of it. Most of the Ṣaḥāba had departed by the departure of the rightly guided caliphs to the extent that none of the people of Badr remained except for a small number. Most of those who followed them in goodness had departed during the time of the younger Ṣaḥāba — during the rulership of 'Abd Allah b. al-Zubayr and 'Abd al Mālik (b. Marwān). Most of the successors to the tābi'īn departed by the end of the Umayyid dynasty and the beginning of the Abbasid dynasty. **Many non-Arabs became from those appointed to rulership, and much of the affair exited from the rulership of the Arabs. And some of the non-Arab books were translated into Arabic from the books of Persia, India, and Byzantium.** Then what the Prophet صَلَّى ٱللَّهُ عَلَيْهِ وَسَلَّمَ had foretold took place, in as much as that he said:
>
> ثُمَّ يَفْشُو الْكَذِبُ حَتَّى يَشْهَدَ الرَّجُلُ وَلَا يُسْتَشْهَدُ وَيَحْلِفَ وَلَا يُسْتَحْلَفُ
>
> "Then lying will become widespread to such an extent that a man will testify without being requested to testify, and will swear without being asked to swear."
>
> **Then three things transpired: (1.) opinion, (2.) speculative theology (kalām), (3.) and mysticism (taṣawwuf).** Also, tajahhum (the heresy of Jahm b. Ṣafwān) transpired, which is the denial of the (divine) attributes; and anthropomorphism occurred in reaction to that.

The majority of opining (about legal matters) was in Kūfah, being the predominant condition of its dwellers. It was combined with what they had of extreme Shi'ism, as well as an abundance of lying in reporting narrations (ḥadīth). This occurred despite many people of knowledge, truthfulness, and Sunnah existing amongst the best of its inhabitants. However, the intent (here) is that an abundance of lying in narrating, an abundance of opinions in jurisprudence, and Shi'ism in creed existed therein.

Most speculative theology (*al kalām*) and mysticism (*al-taṣawwuf*) was in Baṣrah. In fact, shortly after the deaths of al Ḥasan and Ibn Sirīn, 'Amr b. 'Ubayd and Wāṣil b. 'Aṭā' emerged, as well as those who followed them from the proponents of theological rhetoric and 'itizāl (i.e. the mu'tazilite creed). Also, Aḥmad b. 'Aṭā' al Hujaymī appeared, the companion of 'Abd al Wāḥid b. Zayd, who in turn had been an associate of Al Ḥasan al Baṣrī رَحِمَهُ ٱللَّهُ. He was accompanied by his acolytes from the *Sufīs* and they built a small lodge for the ascetics — the first of its sort built in Islam. 'Abd al-Raḥmān b. Mahdī رَحِمَهُ ٱللَّهُ (135-198 h.) and others called it Al Faqiriyyah. These people used to congregate in a small lodge of theirs.

The (first group) eventually had a method of newly introduced speculative theology that they held with religious conviction, while still holding fast to most other matters of the religion. The other (group) ultimately adhered to a way of innovated worship, while still holding fast to most other matters of legislated worship. The (latter) experienced a spiritual state from (al-simā') meditative listening and (the effect of) sounds to such an extent that one of them would die or fall unconscious. The (former) experienced a spiritual state regarding speech and letters to such an extent their imaginations would take them off into a state of bewilderment. The basis of the affair (of the latter) was speculative theology; whereas, the foundation of the matter of the (former) was pertaining intention. By 'kalām' (i.e., theological speculation), they meant tawḥīd, naming themselves al muwaḥḥidūn (i.e., the monotheists). By 'intention,' the latter also meant tawḥīd, calling themselves the people of tawḥīd and purity.

...Deviation exists in the paths of both the proponents of speculative theological investigation as well as that of the proponents of intention and action when such things are disconnected from following the Messenger.

You find that the books of speculative theology and mysticism originally came out of Baṣrah. The Imams of the Mu'tazilite theology were from Baṣrah, such as Abul Hudhayl al 'Allāf, Abū 'Alī al Jubā'ī and his son Abū Hāshim, Abu 'Abdillah al Ju'l and Abul Ḥussayn al Baṣrī. Likewise was the case with the theologians of the Kullābiyyah and the Ash'ariyyah, such as: 'Abdullah b. Sa'īd b. Kullāb; Abul Hasan al Ash'arī and his counterpart Abul Ḥasan al Bāhilī; al Qāḍī Abu Baker b. Al Bāqilānī and others. Likewise was the case with the books of the Sufis and those who mixed Sufism with hadīth and speculative theology, such as the books of al Ḥārith b. Asad al Muḥāsibī, Abul Ḥasan b. Sālim, Abū Sa'īd al 'Arābī and Abu Ṭālib al Makkī. A good number of people from Baghdād, Khurāsān, and the Levant shared in that with them, but the point is that the originals came from there.[223]

The above passage from Ibn Taymiyyah رَحِمَهُ ٱللَّهُ provides us with a valuable insight into the effects of pseudo-intellectualism and gnostic mysticism in precipitating the fragmenting and weakening of the Muslims. This is because since, as we have priorly illustrated, Islam is built upon (1) simple, knowledge-based, sensible beliefs and (2) loving, venerable compliance to divine commandments, then it follows that any conceptual deviation altering those revealed beliefs, and any practical

[223] Majmū' al Fatāwā, vol. 10, pp. 357-361.

deviation changing the nature of compliance to revealed legislation goes against the very foundation of Islam. Amazingly, the Muslims followed in the footsteps of the previous nations in a manner strikingly similar to what had fragmented them.

Compare the major deviations away from the original simple beliefs and practices of Islam with the relatively identical assessment of Western academics about the correlated formative currents forming the original foundations of Western culture. This will connect the path that the previous nations treaded towards deviance with the path followed by many Muslims to the same ends. Recall the corruptive influences of the Persians and Romans on the Jews and the Christians. Recall that the Muslims were warned by the Messenger Muhammad ﷺ that they would follow the ways of the Persians and the Romans, as well as that of the Jews and the Christians. Recall all that has preceded in the previous chapters about the history of speculative theology and gnostic-mysticism and reconsider the analysis mentioned earlier:

> Western culture is based on the twin pillars of **Greek rationality**, on the one hand, and **biblical faith**, on the other. Certainly, there can be little doubt that these two traditions have been dominant forces in cultural development. The former may be defined by its sole reliance on the rationality of the mind, the latter by its emphasis on an authoritative divine revelation. **However, from the first centuries to the present day there has also existed a third current**, characterized by a resistance to the dominance of either pure rationality or doctrinal faith. **The adherents of this tradition emphasized the importance of inner-enlightenment or gnosis**: a revelatory experience that mostly

entailed an encounter with one's true self as well as with the ground of being, God.[224]

We have previously elaborated on the particulars of this assessment in the last chapters, in which we alluded to the corrosive nature of both Greek philosophy and gnostic-mysticism on the foundation of 'biblical faith.' We identified how these two trends contributed to the alteration of the actual scriptural canon as well as the religious doctrines and rituals of the Jews and Christians.

Bearing this in mind, the dazzling spread of Islam in its earliest days proliferated simple monotheism and moral virtue throughout many areas that were formerly the locus of mysticism, philosophy, and Christianity combined — inexorably placing the Muslims on a trajectory to collide with these volatile doctrines. The intellectual approach that was introduced through Greek philosophy — which insisted on the negation of scripturally substantiated Divine Attributes — rendered Allah unknowable and uninvolved with the world. On the other hand, the emotional approach caused another equally toxic current to spread — one of the Gnostic, Neoplatonic[225] and hermetic[226] variety — whose participants sought after an imaginary oneness of being the Divine — a feat allegedly attainable by rigorous ascetic ritual.

---

[224] van den Broek, R., & Hanegraaff, W. J. (Eds.). (1998). Gnosis and hermeticism from Antiquity to modern times. SUNY (State University of NY) Press. p. vii

[225] Neoplatonism is a philosophical school of thought following Plato's teachings as interpreted by Plotinus (c. 204/5 – 270 ce). Their doctrine is one of monism (a belief in the oneness of existence, i.e. God, Nature, and Man being of one substance).

[226] Hermeticism, also called Hermetism, is a religious, philosophical, and esoteric tradition based primarily upon writings attributed to Hermes Trismegistus ("Thrice Great"). These writings have greatly influenced the Western esoteric tradition and were considered to be of great importance during both the Renaissance and the Reformation. The tradition claims descent from a prisca theologia, a doctrine that affirms the existence of a single, true theology that is present in all religions and that was given by God to man in antiquity. (wikipedia.com)

So, one interpretation rendered Allah as relatively nothing while the other indirectly declared Him as everything; worse yet, the two systems frequently were combined together in a marriage of irreconcilable contradiction—a phenomenon dating back to antiquity. These doctrinal alterations were commonly recognized by generations of orientalists. Previously, we quoted the orientalist, H.A.R. Gibb in this regard, who noted:

> from that point on (i.e. after the passage of four centuries from the advent of Islam), there were two recognized systems of theology in Islam—the transcendentalist and the monist, one that developed to extremes the doctrine of the otherness of God and one that asserted His immanence in every part of nature.[227]

Similarly, Lothrop Stoddard remarked:

> When, however, Islam was accepted by non-Arab peoples, they instinctively interpreted the Prophet's message according to their particular racial tendencies and cultural backgrounds, the result being that primitive Islam was distorted or perverted. The most extreme example of this was in Persia, where the austere monotheism of Muhammad was transmuted into the elaborate mystical cult known as Shiism, which presently cut the Persians off from full communion with the orthodox Muslim world. The same transmutive tendency appears, in lesser degree, in the saint-worship of the North Africa Berbers and in the pantheism of the (Indian) Moslems — both developments which Mohammad would have unquestionably execrated.[228]

Therefore this historical fact is widely documented and conceded to throughout history by Muslims and non-Muslims, despite the efforts of many to normalize and mainstream mystic

---

227 Gibb, H.A.R. (1945); Modern trends in Islam; University of Chicago Press.

228 Stoddard, Lothrop. The New World of Islam, p. 8.

and hyper-rationalist strands of Islam, claiming them to Islamic orthodoxy until this very day.

How Philosophy & Mysticism Directly Contradict the Foundation of Islam

Only by understanding what Islam is can a person appreciate the gravity of this dual threat to the foundation of Islam and thus realize their devastating effects on the fruits of faith. Shaykh al Islām Taqī al-Dīn Aḥmad b. 'Abd al Ḥalīm b. Taymiyyah al Ḥarrānī (رَحِمَهُ ٱللَّهُ) (died 728 h.) said:

> The root of faith is: *qawl al qalb* (the statement of the heart) which is al-taṣdīq (credence and ratification); and *'amal al qalb* (the action of the heart) which is *al maḥabbah* (love) upon the way of *al khuḍū'* (submissiveness) — because the souls of the servants have no affinity as complete as their affinity for their Deity who is Allah, the one whom there is nothing deserving of worship besides. Since īmān (faith) gathers these two concepts (i.e. affirmation of belief and submissive love), and since the expression of those who describe (faith) as only being credence is deficient and lacking, then the Ummah is divided into three groups:
>
> (1) *Al jāmi'ūn* (those who harmonize between) both matters: the (heart's) credence based statement and the (heart's) intention based action. Besides them, there are two groups missing one of these two:
>
> (2) *Al kalāmiyyūn* (the speculative theologians), who overwhelmingly investigate and speak about substantiating or negating, presence or absence, and issues of belief. Their ultimate objective is purely ratification, knowledge, and information.

(3) *Al-ṣūfiyyūn* (the ascetic mystics), whose pursuit and deeds are overwhelmingly in relation to love and hate, intent and aversion, and the action based activities (of the heart). Their ultimate objective is love, compliance, action, and intention.

As for the people of knowledge and faith, then they harmonize between the two affairs: between knowledge-based credence and love-based action. Furthermore, their credence originates from knowledge, just as do their deeds and love. So they are spared from and have eluded the double malady of the deviant speculative theologians and ascetic mystics while acquiring the matter constituting a deficit with both groups.

Each of these deviant groups has two evils. The first: speaking without knowledge, as in the case of the speculative theologian; and acting without knowledge, as in the case of the ascetic mystic. This is what they fell into of innovations in creed and practice that differed with the Book and the Sunnah. The second: action[229] evaded the speculative theologian, whereas statement and speech[230] evaded the ascetic mystic. As for those who are inwardly and outwardly considered *Ahlus-Sunnah*, then their internal and external speech and action occurs by way of knowledge, and both their statements and actions match and merge together. These are the true Muslims.[231]

The Imāms of the Salaf detested speculative theology mainly because it is both harmful and trivial and it does not motivate one to do righteous action — it does not inspire the action and activity of the heart nor the actions of the limbs — as opposed to simple logical beliefs rooted in revelation, which have an immediate connection to loving compliance, upright moral

229 meaning action of the heart and the limbs.

230 meaning speech of the heart (i.e., knowledge and scriptural belief) and the tongue.

231 Majmū' al Fatāwā vol. 2, pp. 40-41. Taḥqīq: 'Abd al-Raḥmān b. Qāsim. Majma' Malik Fahd Printing Complex for the Noble Quran, Al Madinah al-Nabawiyyah, KSA. (1416/1995).

character, and righteous deeds. In contrast to this aforementioned trend of hyper-rationalism, the approach of the Ṣufīs was fundamentally emotive, mostly based on ecstatic passions and 'gnostic' intuition as its foundation; thus it disconnected the vital link between revealed beliefs and loving compliance in the reverse order of speculative theology. Along these lines, the renowned Yemeni scholar, 'Abd ar-Raḥmān al Mu'allimī (رَحِمَهُ ٱللَّهُ) explains further:

> The sources of beliefs associated with Islam are four: two are attributable to the Salaf, namely, the innate disposition and the revealed religion; and two are related to the Khalaf, namely, complicated intellectual investigation and mystic-enlightenment (Ṣufism). (i.) As for innate disposition, then I generally intend thereby: innate guidance, common-sense, and those issues that researchers call self-evident and obvious—within the realm of plausible rational investigation. I also mean by it: that which is easily (comprehended) by illiterates and commoners, who are unacquainted with rhetorical theology or philosophy. (ii.) As for revealed religion, then it is the Book (Qurān) and the Sunnah (Prophetic narrations). (iii.) As for the complicated intellectual investigation, then that is what is related to speculative theology and philosophy. (iv.) As for mystic enlightenment (Ṣufism), then that is well known by its practitioners and sympathizers.[232]

So in the estimation of the Salaf, the fundamentals of religious beliefs were only instinctive logical conclusions substantiated by authentic revealed texts: these constitute the foundation of what is positively orthodox Islam. On the other hand, the later generations who opposed this way split into two directions: one related to understanding and the other related to love and desire, as explained above in the statement of Ibn Taymiyyah. The first was the hyper-rational approach of the

---

[232] Al Mu'allimī; Al Qā'id ilā Taṣḥīḥ al 'Aqā'id p. 37. Al Maktab al Islāmī, 3rd Edition (1404 h./ 1984)

philosophers and speculative theologians, and the second was the approach of the gnostic mystics who sought enlightenment by employing rigorous self-discipline and deprivation.

In his scholarly tome, *Al-Ṣawā'iq al Mursalah*, Ibn al Qayyim (رحمه الله) —defending the simple creed of the earliest Muslims — quotes a lengthy criticism from the *ḥanbalite faqīh* Ibn 'Aqīl (رحمه الله) directed at the dual threat posed by the speculative theologians and gnostic mystics:

> All of them are renegades against the matters of religion: this one audaciously speaks about issues that have explicit scriptural evidence to counter such evidence on behalf of what he claims to be the conclusion of reason; while the other says: my heart has spoken to me on behalf of my Lord... There is nothing more harmful against the religion than the innovating theologians and the ignorant mystics: the (former) corrupt the intellects with speculations and doubts that resemble what is rational; while (the latter) corrupt the deeds.

Ibn al Qayyim comments on the above statement saying:

> This is the speech of one (i.e. Ibn 'Aqīl) who once joined alongside the philosophers to the furthest extent and experienced the epitome of what they possess. He engaged in philosophical speculation and then shunned it, intimately knowing its scope and its furthest bounds.[233]

These dual trends jeopardizing the roots of the tree of faith, namely, philosophy and mysticism, were present long before the advent of Islam, as we have seen. They weakened the beliefs of the previous nations just as they would do to the Muslims. This corruption took hold incrementally, and by the fourth century on

---

233 233 Al-Ṣawā'iq vol. 4, p. 1342-1351

the Islamic calendar, a similar phenomenon as that which had paganized Christendom had befallen the Muslim world.

[The Jahmiyyah]

Al 'Allāmah 'Abd al-Raḥmān b. Nāṣir al-Sa'dī (رَحِمَهُ ٱللَّهُ) said in *Tawḍīḥ al Kāfiyah al Shāfiyah*:

> Were you to gather the doctrines of Jahm (78-128 h.) that have been mentioned (by Ibn al Qayyim in the Nūniyyah) which are: (1) negating Allah's attributes; (2) negating His actions; (3) negating His khullah[234] and love; (4) negating His speech and speaking; and (5) negating the actions of the servants — then they necessitate the invalidation of (Allah) creating and commandment, (His) revelation, divine law, and (the elimination of) moral responsibility.
>
> If you were to then add the statement of their Ghulāt (extremest fanatics) as pertains denial of Allah's Beautiful Names to the aforementioned, then you would know that **this doctrine results in the denial and rejection of the Lord of the Worlds.** However, they camouflage and adorn their doctrine. They embellish their phrasing while threatening those who oppose it. Alongside all of that they add slander against the creed of the Salaf and labeling it with repulsive names. That birthed the people's acceptance of it and their yielding to its tribulation — just as the Tribe of Israel succumbed to the trial of the golden calf that had been fashioned and ornamented with beauty. They succumbed to its appearance and glitter just as these people succumbed to embellished speech and ornamented phrases.

[234] Allah's special love for His closest Messengers: the two Khalīls — Ibrahīm and Muhammad عَلَيْهِمَا ٱلسَّلَام.

So the sects of innovation each incorporated something of Jahm's doctrines according to how far away they were from the creed of the Salaf.[235]

Al Maqrīzī (رَحِمَهُ ٱللَّهُ) states in *al Mawā'iẓ wal 'Itibār*:

> Then, after the Era of the *Ṣahābah*, the doctrine of Jahm b. Ṣafwān began in the East, causing great tribulation. For verily, he negated that Allah has any Attributes. He presented the people of Islam with doubts that impacted the Islamic religion with hideous effects, spawning great calamity ever since. This was right before the second Hijri century. He gained many acolytes in his doctrine that amounts to ta'ṭīl (negation of Allah' perfection). The people of Islam abhorred his statement and directed themselves against it, showing their disapproval and declaring its adherents as misguided. They warned against the *Jahmiyyah* and had enmity towards them for Allah's sake, while dispraising whoever sat with them. They wrote that which is well known to the people in refutation of them.[236]

Ibn al Qayyim (رَحِمَهُ ٱللَّهُ) writes in *al-Ṣawā'iq al Mursalah*:

> Once the *Jahmites* appeared at the end of the era of *Tabi'īn*, **they were the first to counterpose the revelation with human reason.** Despite this, they were few, powerless, and dispraised. The first of them was their *Shaikh*, Ja'd bin Dirham who had notoriety with people because he was the teacher and *Shaikh* of Marwān b. Muḥammad. As such, he was called Marwān Al J'adī, in attribution to him. During his tenure, Allah تَبَارَكَ وَتَعَالَىٰ deposed *Banu Umayyah* of their monarchy and rulership, scattering them

[235] Tawḍīḥ al Kāfiyah al-Shāfiyah. Aḍwā' al-Salaf (1420/2000). pp. 27-28.

[236] Al Mawā'iẓ wal i'tibār, p. 190. Al Maqrīzī, Taqī al-Dīn Aḥmad b. 'Alī (845 h.). Al Mawā'iẓ wal I'tibār. Dār al Kutub al 'Ilmiyyah, Beirut (1418).

throughout the land, and utterly shredding them, — owing to the 'blessing' of the *Shaykh* of the *Mu'aṭṭilah* (i.e., the negating rejectors).

Once his (i.e. Ja'd) affair gained popularity amongst the Muslims, he was pursued by Khālid bin 'Abd Allah al Qasrī, the Governor of 'Iraq, who ultimately captured him. On the day of 'Eid al Aḍḥā, he delivered the khuṭbah, concluding it by saying, "Oh people, slaughter your sacrificial animals, for verily I am slaughtering Ja'd bin Dirham. He claimed that Allah did not speak to Moses or take Abraham as a Khalīl (His beloved). Allah is exalted high above what Ja'd purports." Then he came down and slaughtered him at the base of the pulpit, making him his act of sacrifice. Then that tribulation was extinguished.

At that time the people were unanimous about Allah تَبَارَكَ وَتَعَالَى being above His heavens over His throne, apart from His creation, possessing all Attributes of perfection and qualities of Majesty. (They agreed that) He had spoken with actual words to His servant and messenger Moses عَلَيْهِ السَّلَام and showed Himself to the mountain, turning it into dust. This was the state of things until the third century arrived.[237]

Ibn Taymiyyah (رَحِمَهُ ٱللَّهُ) outlines the nature of the Jahmites' misguidance and gives us some important background information about Jahm b. Ṣafwān, the progenitor of their creed:

It was reported from (the Prophet صَلَّى ٱللَّهُ عَلَيْهِ وَسَلَّمَ) that he said about the description of the saved sect: They are whoever is upon what I and my companions are upon today. So (based on what the Jahmites assert) shouldn't he have said that whoever holds fast to the Quran, or to what the Quran points to of meaning, or what is understood from the Quran, or the unambiguous meaning of the Quran in matters of belief is astray? And that guidance lies in your referring back to the analogies of your

[237] Mukhtaṣar al-Ṣawā'iq, vol. 1, p.175.

minds and that which the speculative theologians from amongst you would introduce after the passage of three generations about this doctrine — although its root emerged at the end of the second generation. Furthermore, the source of this doctrine — the doctrine of negating the divine attributes — originated from the protegés of the Jews, polytheists, and deviant Ṣabians. For indeed the first person remembered during the Islamic era that for this doctrine...was al Ja'd b. Dirham. Jahm b. Ṣafwān took it from him and publicized it. Thence the Jahmite doctrine is attributed to him. It has been said that al Ja'd took his doctrine from Abān b. Sam'ān, who took it fromṬālūt, the son of Labīd b. Al 'Aṣam's sister, who, in turn, took it from Labīd b. Al 'Aṣam, the Jewish sorcerer who placed magic on the Prophet.

It is also said about this person, Ja'd (46-105 h.) that he was from the people of Ḥarrān which contained a great deal of Ṣabians and philosophers, who were remnants of the religion of Nimrod and the Canaanites, about whose sorcery some contemporary authors have written ...

This had been their religion (i.e., the people of Harran) before the arrival of Christianity amongst them; later on, Christianity became predominant. However, these polytheistic Ṣabians remained until the advent of Islām, and the Ṣabians and philosophers were found in the Islamic state until the current time. They include the Ṣabians that were in Baghdād and elsewhere who were doctors and authors, some of whom did not become Muslim. When Al Fārābī arrived in Ḥarrān in the fourth (Hijri) century, he held council with them. He learned and accepted from them what had been recieved from the philosophers. Thābit bin Qurrah had written an exposition of Aristotle's speech on theology, which I saw and have explained the corruption that it contained; for indeed, there is a great deal of misguidance therein.

The same was the case of the religion of the people of Damascus before the appearance of Christianity (i.e., they were upon this ancient religion). They used to pray towards the North Pole, and as such you find old Masjids in Damascus with the qiblah (i.e., prayer direction) facing the North Pole. Under the Jāmi' of Damascus (the central masjid), there is a large temple erected that previously belonged to these people with the North Pole as its prayer niche.

In as much as that the origin of Jahm's doctrine is the statement of the Ṣabian distorters — who are worse than the Jews and Christians — then the Imāms said that their doctrine is worse than that of the Jews and Christians. Nonetheless, they are better than the pure polytheists, the likes of whom Jahm debated —those who deny the existence of a maker or who mandate worshipping another deity. These specific Ṣabians were not like that. However, although they do not mandate polytheism, they concurrently do not forbid it. Instead, they permit both monotheism and polytheism. They approve of the worship performed by both the monotheists and the associationists simultaneously, without rejecting either, as is present in their speech.

The Ṣabians at that time, to the exception of a small minority, were upon polytheism and their scholars were philosophers, although it was possible for a Ṣabian to believe in Allah and the Last Day as opposed to being a polytheist. However, many, or most of them, were disbelievers or polytheists in the same manner as how many Jews and Christians had altered and distorted (their religion), thus becoming disbelievers or associationists. These particular Ṣabians were, at that time, disbelieving associationists worshipping planets and building temples devoted to them.

The Nufāt (lit. deniers, i.e., negative theologians) from them believed about God that He is only describable with attributes of negation, or of ownership, or a combination of the two. **They are the same ones that Abraham al Khalīl (عَلَيْهِ السَّلَام) was (previously) sent to**. So Ja'd took from the Ṣabian philosophers. Likewise Abū Naṣr al Fārābī (260-339 h.)[238] entered Ḥarrān and took the completion of his philosophy from the Ṣabian philosophers. Jahm (78-128 h.) also took (his belief) from them, when he debated the *Samniyyah* —some Indian philosophers that reject that anything can be positively known except by way of the senses — as Al Imām Aḥmad (164-241h.) and others have mentioned. **These are Jahm's chains of transmission tracing back to the Jews, Ṣabians, polytheists, and astray philosophers who themselves were either *Ṣabians* or pagan associationists. So the misguided philosophers are either from the Ṣabians or from the pagan associationists.**[239]

[The Mu'tazilah]

Al Maqrīzī (رَحِمَهُ ٱللَّهُ) continues:

[238] Abu Naṣr Muhammad b. Muhammad al Fārābī, is known in the West as Alpharabius; (c. 872 – 951/ c. 350 h.) was a popular philosopher and jurist who wrote in the fields of political philosophy, metaphysics, ethics and logic. He was also a scientist, cosmologist, mathematician and music scholar. In Arabic philosophical tradition, he is known with the title "the Second Teacher", after Aristotle being known in the East as "the First Teacher". He is credited with preserving the original Greek texts during the Middle Ages because of his commentaries and treatises, and influencing many prominent philosophers, like Avicenna (Ibn Sinā)and Maimonides.

[239] Majmū' al Fatāwā vol 5, pp. 20-22.

In the interim, the creed of the Mu'tazilah began, in the third Hijri century — in continuation from the time of al Ḥasan b. Al Ḥussayn al Baṣrī (رَحِمَهُ ٱللَّهُ). They wrote about some issues such as justice, tawḥīd, and affirmation of people's actions while asserting that Allah did not create what is bad, and they were ignorant about (the believers') seeing Allah's in the Hereafter. They denied the body's punishment in the grave and proclaimed that the Quran is created and man-made, as well as many other issues. Many people followed them in their innovations, writing exhaustively and employing methods of speculative theology in support of their doctrine. So the Imams of Islam forbade their doctrine and dispraised speculative theology. They ostracized whoever practiced it. However, the affair of the Mu'tazilah continually strengthened, their acolytes increased, and their doctrine spread throughout the earth.[240]

Likewise, Ibn al Qayyim (رَحِمَهُ ٱللَّهُ) continues in *al-Ṣawā'iq*:

Allah's slave M'amūn became the ruler, and he loved an assortment of sciences. He held private council on the sciences with all sorts of speculators. Obsession with rationalizations overwhelmed him, so he ordered the Arabization of the Greek books and brought translators from the provinces. So they were translated and Arabized, upon which the people preoccupied themselves with them. Rulership is a market, whatever is lucrative will be procured therein. Some of the *Jahmites* — who his brother Al Amīn had banished and searched for to kill or capture — now dominated his privileged audience. They filled his ears and heart with the heresy of *Jahmism*, which he accepted and approved of. He then called the people to it and meted out punishment on its behalf. His period did not remain for long. The affair transferred to Al Mu'taṣim after him. It was

240 Al Mawā'iẓ wal i'tibār, vol. 4, p. 190.

he that lashed Imām Aḥmad bin Ḥanbal. So he (i.e. Al Mu'taṣim) established the propagation in succession while the *Jahmites* approved of his actions, encouraging them and telling him that he was exonerating Allah from anthropomorphism and embodiment by doing so. They overwhelmingly constituted his private audience and close advisors, so much so that the judges and governors were selected from them, in as much as that they (customarily) follow in accordance to their kings.[241]

Elsewhere Ibn Taymiyyah رَحِمَهُ ٱللَّهُ elaborates:

> Later, when the Roman (Byzantine) books were Arabized in the second century, the tribulation was exacerbated beyond what Satan had cast into the hearts of the misguided — which was of the same sort of what he had previously cast into the hearts of their counterparts. During the second century, this belief — that the Salaf termed the Jahmite creed — spread by way of Bishr b. Ghayāth al Marīsī (138-218 h.) and his generation. There is a great deal of speech dispraising them and declaring their misguidance from the Imāms such as Mālik (bin Anas), Sufyān b. 'Uyaynah, ('Abd Allah) bin Al Mubārak, Abū Yusuf, Al-Shāfi'ī, Aḥmad (bin Ḥanbal), Isḥāq bin (Rahawayh), al Fuḍayl b. 'Iyyāḍ, Bishr (b. Ḥārith) al Ḥāfī, and others. The misinterpretations available in people's hands today are the same misinterpretations mentioned by Bishr al Marīsī in his book. Such is the case with most of the misinterpretations of Abū Bakr bin Fawrak in the book Al-T'awīlāt, those mentioned by Abū 'Abd Allāh Muḥammad bin 'Umar al-Rāzī in the book he named Ta'sīs al-Taqdīs, and that which exists in the speech of many other people besides them such as Abū 'Alī al Jubā'ī, 'Abd al Jabbār b. Aḥmad al Hamadhānī, Abū al Ḥussayn al Baṣrī, Abu al Wafā' b. 'Aqīl, Abū Ḥāmid al Ghazālī and others.

[241] Mukhtaṣar al-Ṣawā'iq, vol. 1, pp.175-176.

However, the outright rejection of t'awīl (reinterpreting Divine Attributes) and other good things can be found in some of their speech. I merely have clarified here that their exact misinterpretations are exactly the same as Al Marīsī's misinterpretations. This is proven by the book of refutation written by 'Uthmān bin Sa'īd al-Dārimī (d. 280 h.), one of the well-known Imams during Bukhārī's time. He wrote a book, calling it, *'Uthman bin Sa'īd's Refutation Upon the Obstinate Liar Pertaining what he Fabricated Against Allah as Relates Monotheism.* He reported the exact same misinterpretations from Bishr al Marīsī with speech that conclusively showed that Al Marīsī was actually more principled and knowledgeable about textual evidence and logic then these latter-day persons whose misinterpretations had arrived at them from him initially. 'Uthmān bin Sa'īd proceeded to refute that with speech that once seen would convince any logical sensible person about the reality of what the Salaf were upon, the clarity of the evidence for their method, and the weakness of the opponents' evidence.[242]

Ibn al Qayyim says:

Despite all of that, they (i.e., the Mu'tazilites) did not have the audacity to invalidate the scriptural texts and grant primacy to human reason and opinions above them. Islam was still in a state of preeminence and power. The market for ḥadīth was lucrative and the luminaries of the Sunnah were still on the surface of the earth. However, they were grazing in close proximity to such things and were muttering them inaudibly. Through enticement and terror they seized upon the people. Some blindly responded affirmatively and some, under duress, gave in to what they wanted so as to ransom themselves, while their hearts remained at peace with faith. Allah تَبَارَكَ وَتَعَالَى made the hearts of some people firm in defense of His religion, rendering

[242] Al Fatwā al Ḥamawiyyah al Kubrā. Taqī al-Dīn Ahmad b. 'Abdul Ḥalīm b. Taymiyyah al Ḥarrānī (728 h.). Dar al-Ṣamī'ī, Riyāḍ. 2nd edition (1425/2004). See: p. 241-251. Majmū' al Fatawā, vol. 5. p. 22-23.

them stronger than stone and mightier than iron. He established them to defend His religion and made them Imams for the believers to pattern themselves after owing to their patience and certainty about Allah's evidences. For certainly, by patience and certainty leadership in the religion is attained.

﴿وَجَعَلْنَا مِنْهُمْ أَئِمَّةً يَهْدُونَ بِأَمْرِنَا لَمَّا صَبَرُوا وَكَانُوا بِآيَاتِنَا يُوقِنُونَ﴾

"We made them leaders, guiding others by Our command once they had been patient and were certain of our clear signs."[243]

So they were patient over the Jahmites' severe abuse. They did not abandon the *Sunnah* of Allah's Messenger because of the enticing incentives or because of the terrorizing threats.

Allah (تَبَارَكَ وَتَعَالَىٰ) then extinguished this tribulation and suppressed that doctrine. He aided the Sunnah with a mighty victory and granted its people a clear triumph until it was proclaimed loudly from atop the pulpits and invited to in every Bedouin region and hometown. During that era, books of Sunnah were authored to such an extent that only Allah (تَبَارَكَ وَتَعَالَىٰ) fully knows. Then that era and its people passed away. Their offspring stood in their wake, inviting to Allah's book and His Messenger's Sunnah (صَلَّى ٱللَّهُ عَلَيْهِ وَسَلَّمَ) with insight, up until there emerged what none were able to prevent, the true legion of the devil — those who war against what the Messengers brought by way of their reasoning and opinions. Namely, they were the *Qirāmiṭah* and atheistic *Bāṭiniyyah* (esotericists). They invited mankind to the human reason alone, saying that the matters taken from the Messengers disagreed with human reason. It is they who truly established this trajectory in word and deed.[244]

[The Mushabbihah]

Al Maqrīzī (رَحِمَهُ ٱللَّهُ) continues:

[243] Al-Sajdah: 24

[244] Mukhtaṣar al-Ṣawā'iq, vol. 1, p.176.

Then, in counteraction to the Mu'tazilite doctrine, the doctrine of anthropomorphism began. Muhammad b. Karrām b. 'Arāq b. Ḥizābah, the leader of the Karrāmiyyah sect emerged two hundred years after the hijrah. He affirmed the existence of Divine Attributes to the extreme of asserting anthropomorphism. He left for pilgrimage, arrived in the Levant and died in Zaghrah in the month of Ṣafar 251 h. He was buried at al Maqdis. He had over twenty thousand followers there engaged in worship and asceticism besides those in the East who were innumerable in multitude. He was an Imam for a group of Shāfi'is and Ḥanafis. There were many debates, disagreements, and multiple incidents of civil strife between the Karrāmiyyah and the Mu'tazilah in the East.[245]

The Persian Retribution

Alongside the broader philosophical and mystical trends discussed previously, Al Maqrīzī (رحمه الله) also highlights another ancient threat that served as the source of much of the heterodoxy and heresy that fragmented the Muslim world until today. He writes:

> Know that the cause of the departure of most sects away from the religion of Islam is that the Persians once had widespread rulership and a hand of authority above all nations. They deemed themselves to be majestic, in as much as that they used to call themselves the free-men and masters while considering all other people to be their slaves. So after the tribulation of the losing their nation at the hands of the Arabs — who the Persians viewed as being the least significant of all peoples — they were overwhelmed by this, which only exacerbated the calamity to them. So they, in turn, launched a plan to attack Islam at

[245] Al Mawā'iẓ wal i'tibār, vol. 4, p. 190.

intermittent times — throughout which Allah (تَبَارَكَ وَتَعَالَىٰ) always gave victory to the truth...

Some of their people outwardly converted to Islam and won over the adherents to *Shi'ism* by outwardly feigning love for Ahl al Bayt (i.e., the household of the Prophet), and repulsion of Ali being oppressed. Then they led them down many pathways until they removed them from the path of guidance. They involved some of them in purporting that there is a man waiting to emerge called the Mahdi who has the reality of the religion, because it is not allowed to accept the religion from unbelievers. This is because they attributed unbelief to the Companions of Allah's Messenger. Another group of people exited by claiming prophethood for some people that they named as such. The took other people into the belief in al ḥulūl and the inapplicability of the laws. They meddled with some other people, obligating fifty daily prayers for them, while others said that it is really seventeen prayers, each of which consists of ten units, which was the statement of 'Abd Allah b. 'Amr b. Al Ḥārith al Kindi, before he became a Safri kharijite.

The Jewish 'Abd Allah b. Saba' al Ḥimyarī feigned conversion to Islam in order to plot against its people. So he was the root of inciting the people against 'Uthmān b. 'Affān. 'Ali immolated a group of them when they declared him as divine. It was from these roots that the Ismā'iliyyah and the Qirāmiṭah originated.[246]

It is worth noting the level of depravity and licentiousness that Persia had sunken into in the centuries before the advent of Islam. Recall the statement previously quoted by American historian Lothrop Stoddard, who was actually fond of the Persian-Iranian interpretation of Islam:

---

[246] Al Mawā'iẓ wal i'tibār, vol. 4, p. 198

> When, however, Islam was accepted by non-Arab peoples, they instinctively interpreted the Prophet's message according to their particular racial tendencies and cultural backgrounds, the result being that primitive Islam was distorted or perverted. The most extreme example of this was in Persia, where the austere monotheism of Muhammad was transmuted into the elaborate mystical cult known as Shiism, which presently cut the Persians off from full communion with the orthodox Muslim world... developments which Mohammad would have unquestionably execrated.[247]

As Muslim and non-Muslim historians have accurately assessed, many of the Shi'ite doctrines were simply a repurposing and continuation of Persian religion. The dualism of Zoroastrianism is well known, with its belief in a transcendent 'God' of good and a second 'God' of evil—which ultimately lent itself to tyrannical utopian communist schemes of redistributing property and wealth—which is a main current of thought permeating both ancient and modern gnosticism.[248] Ibn al Qayyim (رَحِمَهُ ٱللَّهُ) says in Ighātha al-Lahfān:

> The Magians (latter-Zoroastrians) revere light, fire, water and earth. They profess belief in in the prophethood of Zoroaster. They have distinct religious laws which they follow and they consist of many sects. From these (sects) are the Mazdakites (a fifth century CE movement in Iran), the acolytes of Mazdak, a mobad, meaning an exemplary priest. They believe in communally sharing women and earnings in the same manner that they share air, public pathways, etc.

Likewise, the heresiographer, Al-Shahrastānī (رَحِمَهُ ٱللَّهُ) said:

---

[247] The New World of Islam, p. 8.

[248] As discussed by Voegelin in Science, Politics, and Gnosticism, and by many others.

> Mazdak forbade people from differing, hatred and fighting. Because most of that happens entirely due to women and wealth, he was permissive pertaining women and wealth—making all people partners in both, just as they share water, fire and foliage.[249]

The exemplary scholar and historiographer of Islam, Abū Ja'far Al-Ṭabarī (رَحِمَهُ ٱللَّهُ) explains further:

> The lowest people mandated that, simultaneously exploiting and supporting Mazdak and his acolytes. The people faced tribulation by them; their affair grew to such strength that they would enter upon a man in his home and overtake his home, women and wealth. He would be rendered incapable of defending himself against them. They forced (the King) to declare it justified, threatening to depose him otherwise. They remained in such a condition for only a short time until a man would not know his child, nor a child its father, and until a man could not own anything meaningful.[250]

It was this prevalence of depraved behavior that resulted in the decay and collapse of the Persian empire. It was also from this very backdrop of philosophy, mysticism, and licentiousness that the savage esoteric sects emerged to threaten the Muslim world, leading it to its decline.

---

[249] Al-Shahrastānī. Al Milal wal-Niḥal, Vol. 1, p. 249.

[250] Tārīkh al-Ṭabari, p. 58.

[The Bāṭiniyyah]

Al Maqrīzī (رحمه الله) writes about the emergence of the militant esotericists known as the Bāṭiniyyah who ravaged the Muslim world:

> Besides this, the affair of the *Shi'ite* spread amongst the people until the doctrine of the *Qirāmiṭah* transpired. They are attributed to Ḥamdān al Asha'th who was known as Qirmaṭ owing to his short stature, small legs, and stunted pace. The affair of this man Qirmaṭ began in the year 264 h.[251] He appeared in the darkness of Kufah, and his creed gained popularity in Iraq. In the Levant, Ṣāḥib al Khāl,[252] Al Mudathir,[253] and Al Muṭawwaq,[254] from the Qirāmiṭah arose. In Baḥrayn, Abu Sa'īd al Janābī, from the people of Janābah, arose. His State became great, as did that of his sons after him, to such an extent that they attacked the armies of Baghdad and terrorized the Abbasid Caliphs. They forced tribute on the people of Baghdād, Khurāsān, the Levant, Egypt, and Yemen — which was to be delivered to them annually. They also attacked

---

[251] Ḥamdān b. Al Ash'ath, nicknamed Qirmaṭ, a nickname describing his short stature. He was initially from Khūzastān in the province of Al Ahwāz and later relocated to Al Kūfah. His cult relied upon secret military organization. On the outside, they professed Shi'ism and an ascription to Muḥammad b. Ismā'īl b. J'afar al-Ṣādiq. From the inside, their cult was based on atheistic philosophy, immorality, destruction of virtue and an effort to destroy the Islamic rulership. Their movement initially spread by way of 'Abdullah b. Maymūn al Qadāḥ, who spread the teachings of the extremist, heretical Ismā'iliyyah throughout the south of Persia around the year 260 h. Eventually their influence spread to 'Irāq and in 278 h. Ḥamdān Qirmaṭ b. Al Ash'ath openly promoted their cult near Kufah.

[252] A moniker for the Qirmaṭī leader Aḥmed b. 'Abdullah who claimed Imamite and lineage directly back to Ali through Ja'far al-Ṣādiq. His army was defeated and he was publicly executed by Al Muktafī in the year 291 h.

[253] A moniker for a man named Hussayn, who was the paternal uncle of the aforementioned Aḥmed b. 'Abd Allah al Qirmaṭī, who claimed to be the Mahdī.

[254] A moniker for a young man from the family of the so-called Mudathir. He was charged with the task of killing the Muslim captives. He massacred many men, women, and children in many towns. See Al Kāmil fi'l-Tārīkh vol. 6. p. 417-418.

> Baghdād, the Levant, Egypt, and the Ḥijāz. Their call spread throughout the territories of the earth, whereupon communities of people joined their da'wah and had an affinity towards their doctrine, which they called *'ilm al bāṭin* (esoteric knowledge) — which was a reinterpretation of the laws of Islam and verses of the Qurān. They redirected (the verses) away from their apparent meanings to matters that they purported from themselves. They claimed farfetched interpretations for verses of the Quran that they fabricated, innovating them based on their whims. So they strayed and set many in the world astray.[255]

Later on he writes:

> The truth about which there is no doubt is that Allah's religion is apparent in meaning, having nothing hidden therein. It is pure, not having any secret under it. The entirety of it is binding on every person and is not optional. Allah's Messenger (ﷺ) did not conceal as much as a word of the religion. He did not give the closest people to him — not a wife, nor a child — a privileged look at something that he hid from the red or black complected or from the sheepherders. Allah's Messenger (ﷺ) did not have a secret or a code or any esoteric hidden knowledge. He only had that to which he invited all of humankind. Had he concealed something, then he would not have conveyed (the message of Islam) as commanded. Whoever asserts this, then he is an unbeliever by the consensus of the Ummah.[256]

Ibn al Qayyim (رَحِمَهُ ٱللَّهُ), continuing his chronology of the development of these innovated aberrations, says:

> Thereupon the *Qirāmiṭah Baṭiniyyah* did what they did to the religion. They inclined a great deal to the way of the corruptive

[255] Al Maqrīzī. Al Mawā'iẓ wal i'tibār, vol. 4, p. 190.

[256] ibid, vol. 4, p. 198.

Ṣabians,[257] and during their era *Rasā'il Ikhwān al-Ṣafā*[258] was written. Ibn Sīnā[259] mentioned that his father was from the Egyptian proponents of their *da'wah*. At that time, they ruled over Egypt, having conquered it. Ibn Sīnā said that because they believed in philosophy, that he busied himself with that. Beyond these, a substantial degree of *tajahhum*[260] appeared.

Thereupon, what tragically befell the Muslims occurred, the army of the Khalīfah was ravaged multiple times, they murdered Ḥujjāj (i.e., those traveling for Ḥajj) extensively. Then they reached Makkah itself, killed the arriving pilgrims and removed the black stone. Their power grew exponentially, their affair became exacerbated, the direness of the situation was terrible, and the tribulation they caused was severe. **The foundation of**

---

257 The "corruptive Ṣabians" is a reference to the syncretic philosophies of the cosmological civilizations of Chaldea and Mesopotamia predating Abraham عَلَيْهِ السَّلَامُ. Their history was discussed in an earlier chapter and their influence on the Muslim world has been discussed throughout this book.

258 These fifty-odd essays of the so-called brethren of purity mixed Greek philosophy and occult esoteric beliefs together alongside aspects of Islamic creed. They were an extension of the Ismā'iliyyah and were one of the first esoteric groups to use Shi'ism and Sufism as a mask to spread atheistic teachings that aimed at disposing of Islamic rule and accommodating pre-Islamic paganism, Zoroastrianism and immorality. They first appeared in Baṣrah during the second half of the fourth century hijri. They were proponents of the belief in monism (the perpetual oneness of the Creator with the creation) and the belief in the infallibility of the Shi'ite Imām.

259 Ibn Sīnā, was a famous polymath (370-428 h./980-1037 CE) who authored many books on medicine, philosophy and theology. Alongside his philosophical and theological inclinations, he was a Shi'ite in creed. The historiographer of Islam, al Ḥāfiẓ Al Dhahabī and Al Ḥāfiẓ Ibn Ḥajr both said about him: He is the philosopher of the religion, and he is astray. Ibn Ḥajr said: May Allah not be pleased with him. Ibn Ṣalāḥ said: He wasn't from the scholars of the Muslims but rather he was a human devil. Ibn Al Ḥamawī al-Shāfi'ī said after listing the heretical beliefs of Ibn Sīnā: The scholars of his time and those Imāms thereafter whose statements about the fundamentals and branches (of Islam) hold consideration were unequivocal in declaring his unbelief as well as the unbelief of Abū Naṣr al Fārābī because of their belief in these issues and that differing from the beliefs of the Muslims. Ibn Kathīr said that Al Ghazālī declared him a disbeliever for saying that: the universe is eternal; the denial of physical resurrection for Judgment Day; the denial that Allah knows the details of things. Ibn Taymiyyah famously refuted Ibn Sīnā in the books Naqḍ al Manṭiq, Dar' al-Ta'āruḍ and elsewhere in his writings. Some say that he repented at the end of his life.

260 i.e. the teachings popularized by Jahm b. Ṣafwān

their way is that intellect contrasts what the Messengers brought, and so when logic and revelation conflict, we are to grant precedence to logic.[261]

The Catalyst of the Ideological Attack: the Arabization of the Books of Philosophy

We have already recounted the events surrounding the translation of the books of philosophy into Arabic. This is an event that warrants further attention as pertains the history of deviation. Al Maqrīzī (رَحِمَهُ ٱللَّهُ) backtracks in his narrative of events to clearly outline the definitive ideological origin of these enormous tribulations leading to unmistakable historical crisis for the civilization of the Muslim world. He says (رَحِمَهُ ٱللَّهُ):

> Furthermore, the seventh Abbasid Caliph in Baghdād was Al M'amūn 'Abd Allah b. Hārūn al-Rashīd.[262] Having a passionate love for ancient knowledge, then a few odd years after 210 he sent those who would translate into Arabic and retrieve the books of philosophy to Byzantium. The doctrines of the philosophers circulated amongst the people and their books gained popularity throughout most of the territories. **The *Mu'tazilah*, the *Qirāmiṭah*, the *Jahmiyyah*, and others focused their attention upon them, researching them and perusing their pages. Indescribable calamity and tribulation in religion were dragged across the Muslim world and its people from the studies of philosophy.** The misguidance of the people of innovation was exacerbated by way of philosophy, which increased them in (further) unbelief in addition to (preexistent) unbelief.[263]

---

[261] Mukhtaṣar al-Ṣawā'iq, vol. 1, pp.176-177.

[262] 170-218 h./ 786-833 CE. He ruled for around twenty years until dying at the age of 48.

[263] Al Mawā'iẓ wal i'tibār, vol. 4, p. 191.

In identical fashion Ibn al Qayyim identifies the ancient origins of the crisis of Islam and the Muslims. He says:

> It is purported that Aristotle altered the way of the Ṣabians preceding him that had once believed in Allah and the Last Day, as the Qurān had commended them. His origin was from the associationists and the corruptive *Ṣabians* of India and Greece. He was from those who transformed the Jews, who were people of scripture. Ja'd bin Dirham and then, later on, Jahm bin Ṣafwān and their followers took this (doctrine) from them (the Ṣabian philosophers). **Right before, during, and after the year two hundred, the books of the Greeks were brought from the Byzantine Christian lands and Arabized, upon which the creed of the Ṣabian corrupters like Aristotle and his supporters spread.** During that time the *Kharamiyyah* sect appeared who were the first *Bāṭiniyyah Qirāmiṭah*. They had internally adopted some of the religion of the corruptive Ṣabians while also incorporating the Magian religion — utilizing the speech of the former about the soul and reason while using the rhetoric of the latter about darkness and light. **They clothed that with other phrases, refashioned it and presented it to the Muslims.**[264]

{The Subsequent Proliferation of the Deviant Sects}

Al Maqrīzī (رحمه الله) then explains how the spread of philosophy that the translation movement initiated, gave way to the proliferation of the deviant sects and how the people of Sunnah then became an extreme minority in the Muslim territories. He writes:

> When the Buwayhid dynasty — who publicly asserted the doctrine of the Shi'ite — was established in

264

Baghdād in the year 334 h., continuing until the year 437, the Shi'ite were strengthened. They wrote: "May Allah curse Mu'awiyyah b. Abī Sufyān, as well as whoever angered Fāṭimah, whoever prevented al Ḥussayn from being buried with his grandfather, whoever banished Abu Dharr, and whoever removed al 'Abbās from the advisory council" on the doors of the Masjids in the year 351. During the night, some people tore it off. So, with the permission of Mu'izz al-Dawlah (the ruler), the vizier Muhallabi advised them to write, "May Allah curse whoever oppressed Ahl al Bayt" not designating anyone name in the curse except for Mu'awiyyah. This resulted in great civil strife between the Sunni and Shi'ite in Baghdad. The Shi'ite in Karkh (i.e., the western neighborhood of Baghdad) also publicly added "Ḥayya 'alā khayril 'amal" (lit. come to the best action — intending thereby allegiance to the twelve Imams) to the adhān.

Beyond that, the doctrine of the Mu'tazilah spread throughout 'Irāq, Khurasān, and Transoxiana.[265] Many of the well-known jurists then adopted it as their doctrine. Along with that, the affair of the Fatimid caliphs became powerful in Africa and Morocco. They publicized the *Ismā'īlī* doctrine and dispatched the propagators of their call to Egypt. Many of its people were responsive to their call. Later, in the year 358 H. they gained rule over it and sent their armies into the Levant. Thereupon the doctrines of the Rāfiḍah popularly spread throughout most of the land: al-Maghrib, Egypt, the Levant, the provinces of the Banū Bakr, Kufah, Baṣrah, and Baghdad, as well as all of Iraq, Khurāsān, Transoxiana, and even as far as the Ḥijāz, Yemen, and Bahrain. Frequent civil

[265] literally the land beyond the [Oxus] River. i.e. the eastern lands such as Bukhara, Samarqand, etc.

strife, warring, and skirmishing occurred between them and the Sunnis to an immeasurable degree.

> Additionally, the doctrines of the various sects of the *Qadariyyah*, the *Jahmiyyah*, the *Mu'tazilah*, the *Karrāmiyyah*, the *Khawārij*, the *Rāfiḍah*, the *Qirāmiṭah*, and the *Bāṭiniyyah* became widespread in popularity until they filled the earth. There was not a single one of them except that they researched philosophy and followed its methods according to personal preference. Not a single territory or province remained except that it comprised of many groups of those who we have mentioned.[266]

We have seen from this narrating of events that the Muslim world was fragmented along preexistent sectarian lines that had been widened substantially by the translation of the books of Greek philosophy and of other toxic creeds. These ideological fault lines gave way to an avalanche of devastation for the Muslim world unlike anything seen before.

The Crusades & Mongol Invasions

Ibn al Qayyim (رَحِمَهُ ٱللَّهُ) concludes the sequence of deviations that led to the crisis and decline of Islamic civilization. He says:

> During their time (i.e., the time where the Bāṭinī sects, the Faṭimids, and the Rāfiḍah ruled most of the Muslim world) the disbelievers gained control of many Muslim lands in the East and the West. The pillar of Islām nearly toppled had it not been for the defense of the One that guaranteed its preservation until Allah (تَبَارَكَ وَتَعَالَىٰ) inherits the earth and all that are upon it. Thereafter, their *da'wah* smoldered in the east and appeared in

[266] Al Mawā'iẓ wal i'tibār, vol. 4, p. 191.

the west to a small degree, initially. The situation then exacerbated; then they gained power and their people gained control over much of the Maghreb. They proceeded throughout the land until they reached the land of Egypt, took rulership of it and built the city of Cairo. They, their governors and their judges explicitly established their *d'awah* therein. It was during their time that the *Rasā'il Ikhwān al-Ṣafā* was written as well as *Al Ishārāt*[267], *Al-Shifā*[268] and the books of Ibn Sīnā, who used to say: My father was from the adherents of the *Ḥākamiyyah*[269] *da'wah*. The Sunnah and its books were discarded en masse in their time, except in secrecy. The slogan of their d'awah was giving precedence to human reason above revelation.

They gained authority over the land of Morocco, Egypt, the Levant, and the Ḥijāz. They conquered 'Irāq for a year and treated the people of Sunnah as more inferior than that of Ahl al-Dhimmah (i.e. protected non-Muslim residents) amidst the Muslims at large. Rather, the protected non-Muslim residents had pacts of non-aggression, status, and dignity that the people of Sunnah did not. How many of their swords were plunged into the necks of scholars? How many inheritors of the Prophets died in their prisons?

This remained until Allah (تَبَارَكَ وَتَعَالَى) rescued Islām and the Muslims with Nūr al-Dīn (Al-Zankī)[270] and his nephew Ṣalāḥ al-Dīn[271]. Allah (تَبَارَكَ وَتَعَالَى) resuscitated Islām from its malady after it had prepared itself for condolences. It thrived once again after longstanding obscurity until the inhabitants of the heavens and

---

[267] Al Ishārāt wal-Tanbīhāt was written by Ibn Sinā and later explained by the heretical Nuṣayr al-Dīn al-Ṭūsī

[268] Another book of Ibn Sinā filled with teachings antithetical to Islamic creed.

[269] meaning the political movement of the so-called Faṭimiyyah

[270] 511-569 h. / 1118-1174 ce

[271] 532-589 h. / 1138-1193 ce

earth rejoiced. Its moon shown full once again after having entered the phase of invisibility. Its soul rushed back into it after having reached the collarbone (nearly departing), and the performer of Ruqyah being summoned. Allah (تَبَارَكَ وَتَعَالَىٰ) rescued the *Bayt al Maqdis* from the hands of cross worshippers with His servant and army. Each supporter of Allah and His Messenger took a fair share of the effort. The creed of the Sunnah was exalted and announced publicly to the masses and a caller announced: Oh supporters of the Sunnah do not disband from the struggle for verily it is the most extensive provision for the day of Judgment.

The people lived in that light for a period of time until darkness overwhelmed the East. They had granted precedence to opinions, human reason, politics, and mystical experience over the divine revelation. Philosophy, speculative theology and its peripheral topics became commonplace. Thereupon, Allah تَبَارَكَ وَتَعَالَىٰ sent against them slaves endowed with propensity for extraordinary harm (i.e., the Tatar/Mongol hoards) by which they penetrated the innermost parts of their dwellings, reaping havoc throughout the villages and provinces. The very name of Islām nearly vanished and all semblance of it was nearly erased.

The instigator and scholar of this tribulation, to whom it is all traceable — its protagonist that it depended upon was the chief of all of the chieftains of those who counterpoised the human reason with revelation. Their Imām in that era was Naṣīr al-Shirk and Kufr (the supporter of polytheism and disbelief, namely Naṣīr al-Dīn Muḥammad bin Muḥammad Al-Ṭūsī.[272] He was unparalleled by his contemporaries in his popularly counterpoising between human reason and revelation, attempting thereby to completely disprove the revelation. For certainly, he established the call to philosophy and took *Al Ishārāt* (of Ibn Sinā) as a replacement for (Quranic) chapters and verses. He said that there are proven logicalities that oppose

272 [597-692 h.]

instructive revelations. He subjected the people of Islām and the scholars of faith to sword, not sparing any except those that escaped him, intentionally trying to abolish the call to Islam. He transferred control of the Muslims' religious schools and endowments to vile sorcerers, necromancers, philosophers, atheists, and speculative theologians. He believed that the call to prayer should be abolished and that the prayer should be redirected toward the North pole. He was obstructed from doing so by the One (i.e., Allah) Who had guaranteed to preserve and defend Islām. All of this is the fruit of those that conflicted between the intellect and revelation.

Make sure that you remember the story of their ancient chieftain at all times (i.e. *Iblīs*). He was the first to counter revelation with human reason, granting precedence to the intellect. His affair ended up exactly as Allah (تَبَارَكَ وَتَعَالَىٰ) narrated. **This chieftain passed on this conflict as a legacy to his students. Ever since, every trial and tribulation for the Prophets and their followers has emanated therefrom.** The basis of of every calamity in the universe, is as Muḥammad al-Shahrastānī stated: from making revelation disagree with reason and granting precedence to whimsicalities over the religion. **The people are engulfed in the evils of this conflict until the present day.**

Alongside this more recently conflicted shaikh (i.e. al-Ṭūsī), multiple things appeared that were previously unknown, such as the *Ḥissiyyāt* of Al 'Amīdī, the *Ḥaqā'iq* of Ibn 'Arabī,[273] and the skeptical doubts of Al-Rāzī,[274] whereupon the market was

---

[273] The head Ṣūfī, Muḥammad b. 'Alī al-Ṭā'ī al Andalusī 560-638 h. an avid proponent of monism (oneness of existence) and many similar doctrines of clear disbelief.

[274] He died in 606 h. He was considered as one of the greatest Imāms of the Asharis. His immersion into speculative theology drove him to a condition of bewilderment, to such an extent that some of the scholars of Islam declared him an apostate after his writing a book openly promoting polytheism called *Al-Sirr al Maktūm fī al-Siḥr wa Mukhāṭabah al-Nujūm* (the Concealed Secret pertaining Sorcery and Discourse with the Stars). Later in his life he expressed remorse and penitence. Ibn Kathīr and Ibn al Qayyim wrote in many places that he returned back to the way of the early generations at the end of his life.

established for philosophy, rhetoric, and the sciences of the enemies of the Prophets. Then Allah (تَبَارَكَ وَتَعَالَىٰ) looked upon His servants and gave victory to His Book and religion. He established an army to battle the kings of such people with sword and weaponry while establishing an army to battle their scholars with proof and evidence.

Then a trace of them appeared at the head of the seventh century, whereupon Allah (تَبَارَكَ وَتَعَالَىٰ) established Shaikh al Islām Abū al 'Abbās Aḥmad bin Taimiyyah (رَحِمَهُ ٱللَّهُ) (661-728 h.) for His religion, may Allah sanctify his soul. Throughout the duration of his life he undertook battling them with his hand, heart, and tongue. He exposed their falsehood to the people and clarified their misrepresentations and deceptions. He countered them with pure reason and authentic revelation. He healed others while maintaining his own wellness. He clarified their contradiction and their departure from the rule of the very logic they employed as proof and called others to, clarifying to them that they were the greatest abandoners of its rules and judgments. They had neither revelation or logic with them. So he left them perished in their ditches and pierced them with their own arrows. He clarified to them that what was valid of their logicalities serviced the scriptural texts of the Prophets. May Allah (تَبَارَكَ وَتَعَالَىٰ) reward him with tremendous good on behalf of Islām and the Muslims.[275]

---

275 Mukhtaṣar al-Ṣawā'iq, vol. 1, p.177-178.

To bring the crucial point of this volume full circle, reinforcing the entire premise of this book, the esteemed Salafi scholar, Dr. Rabī' b. Hādī 'Umayr al Madkhālī [حفظه الله] stated:

> Then as for (Allah's) statement:
>
> ﴿فَإِمَّا يَأْتِيَنَّكُم مِّنِّي هُدًى فَمَنِ اتَّبَعَ هُدَايَ فَلَا يَضِلُّ وَلَا يَشْقَىٰ﴾
>
> "If guidance comes to you from Me, whomsoever follows My guidance, then he will not stray nor be wretched."[276]
>
> It is a guarantee against misguidance and an emphasized assurance against wretchedness, meaning: (it is) perfect guidance for whoever follows it and is a complete guarantee against humiliating misery in this world and in the hereafter. What humiliation and what wretchedness is more severe than this current humiliation that the Muslims are suffering? What misguidance is more severe than this misguidance that many Muslims are living? Their beliefs oppose Allah's Book. The acts of worship many people engage in oppose the actions of worship that Muḥammad came with, beginning with monotheism in worship (*tawḥīd al 'ubūdiyyah*). (As for) monotheism pertaining the (divine) Names and Attributes (*tawḥīd al asmā' wal-ṣifāt*), then entire schools of thought exist upon something other than Allah's Book and the Sunnah of Allah's Messenger. It has gone so far that some followers of deviant desires who are drowning in misguidance even say: accepting the apparent meanings of the Qurān and Sunnah amounts to polytheism and disbelief![277] This is how far many people have slipped: that they do not believe that complete guidance is found in Allah's Book, so they do not rely upon what Allah said and what Allah's Messenger stated as

---

[276] ṬaHa: 123.

[277] As was expressed by Al-Ṣāwī in his notes on *Tafsīr al Jalālayn*, Surah al Kahf. A number of scholars extensively repudiated his statement, such as Muḥammad al Amīn al-Shinqīṭī in Aḍwā' al Bayān. Refer to his Tafsīr of Surah Muhammad, verse 34.

pertains their beliefs. They believe in the philosophy of the Greeks and in their rhetoric, calling them rationalizations! They distort Allah's Book in favor of these philosophies of Jāhiliyyah that have assaulted us from the West!

Many people imagine that the ideological assault has come about in these latter generations. Rather, the ideological assault came in the earlier generations: from the days in which Aḥmad b. Ḥanbal and his brethren from the people of truth were abused and beaten. Some were even murdered since that time and before. This assault has shaken this Ummah in the most foundational of its fundamentals ever since that time. Philosophical concepts alongside the mysticism of the Magians and (Christian) monks and others have spread since that time. The contemporary assault only came as a completion of the former assault![278]

In conclusion to all that has preceded in the six chapters of this volume, one of the most blatant contemporary examples of today's Culture War and of the continuum of an age-old ideological assault upon the Muslim world exists in a 2003 publication titled Civil Democratic Islam. It, along with many prior and subsequent publications of its type, was issued by the RanD corporation, which is the well-known, Cold War era, policy advising think-tank. Arguably, it is the most influential braintrust consulted about such matters. The contents of this publication are representative of official academic and political attitudes and understandings concerning Islam and Muslims directly bearing impact on the lives of Muslims both in America and far beyond.

In essence, this report — and countless others issued by its contributors and their cohorts — suggests a strategy to identify

---

[278] Excerpted from the article: Wujūb al Ittibā' wal-Taḥdhīr min Maẓāhir al-Shirk wal-Ibtidā'. http://rabee.net/ar/articles.php?cat=11&id=274. Retrieved June 1, 2018/ 15 Ramaḍān 1438 h.

the most widespread interpretations of Islam and direct them to their desired trajectory. It outlines the necessary steps to promote the most 'civil' — in this case synonymous with liberalist and modernist — version(s) to the privileged level of officialdom and orthodoxy, while systematically vilifying so-called 'fundamentalist' interpretations of Islām. Again, here we have the two elements of the historical anti-Islam narrative: (1) vilifying orthodox Islam while (2) promoting their preferred interpretation as a preferable alternative.

In summary, a trend has emerged throughout academia, policy-advising circles, and mass-media of identifying and promoting popular hyper-rational and mystical strands of interpretation. Dating back two centuries to the beginning of the 'modern' era, variations of these alternative interpretations have been focused upon by a kaleidoscope of vested interests. This promotion of a Western preferred interpretation for Islam currently runs parallel to another discourse of similar import: the strategic propaganda that associates the adherents of the original, pure Islamic doctrines and teachings with para-military revolutionary groups patterned upon Western political ideologies.

This series of reports after the tragedy of September 11th was thinly veiled political opportunism to continue the ongoing project of 'westernization' by exploiting Muslim sectarianisms, further dividing the Muslim world — a project inherited by the United States from Western European colonial powers after WWII. These reports merely parrot the legacy of decades of research by the heads of Near Eastern and Islamic studies in the United States and abroad. We have already highlighted the core of their ideology and their understanding of the rise and decline of Muslim civilization in the first chapter of this volume.

Most curiously, they arbitrarily categorize the Muslim world into four clumsy categories: (1) secularists, (2) modernists, (3) traditionalists and (4) fundamentalists. They then assign multiple subcategories to each of these four. They outright dismiss the radical secularists in their report because of their blatant disregard for the most basic of Islamic teachings, relegating their cause into oblivion in the eyes of any self-respecting Muslim. Instead, but not surprisingly, the so-called modernists-liberalists are selected as their candidates and the official representatives of the contemporary 'civilizing mission' to reform Islam and the Muslim world from within. The third category, the 'traditionalists,' is mainly a reference to the uneducated masses who rigidly cling to superstitions and mysticism and who typically have blind-attachment to some variation of one of the four schools of jurisprudence.

The Modernists

The modernist-liberalists have long been the primary focus and loyal pupils of Western ideologues, a tradition dating back for almost two centuries, as the next volume of this work explores. Leonard Binder, an academic at the forefront of such issues, states the dilemma for the westernized modernist-liberalist:

> Faith is not opinion to a true believer. Islam cannot be a matter of opinion. There can be no opinion regarding the theoretical absolute or the revealed truth, though differences may be unavoidable in practice... Liberalism treats religion as opinion and, therefore tolerates diversity in precisely those realms that traditional belief insists upon without equivocation. Islam and liberalism appear to be in contradiction.[279]

[279] Islamic Liberalism (1988) p. 2

Because Islam, quite naturally, is resistant and intolerant of any attack against its fundamentals, as is every viable culture, then the the clear and present danger in the estimation of these self-appointed experts on the Muslim world is that the 'traditionalist' multitudes will incline towards the so-called fundamentalists in forming a bulwark of resistance against ideological encroachment.

Remember that both traditional Western thought and modernity's concept of societal reformation has a default pattern of reaching resolution by means of compromise — endlessly disputing about and trivializing matters of both revelation and logic, until the truth of neither is easily discernible. Recall the assessment of Professor Carrol Quigley who summarized the complexities of Western thought for the uninitiated:

> From this examination of the tradition of the West, we can formulate the pattern of outlook on which this tradition is based. It has six parts: 1. There is a truth, a reality. 2. No person, group, or organization has the whole picture of the truth. (Thus there is no absolute or final authority.) 3. Every person of goodwill has some aspect of the truth, some vision of it from the angle of his own experience. (Thus each has something to contribute.) 4. Through discussion, the aspects of the truth held by many can be pooled and arranged to form a consensus closer to the truth than any of the sources that contributed to it. 5. This consensus is a temporary approximation of the truth, which is no sooner made than new experiences and additional information make it possible for it to be reformulated in a closer approximation of the truth by continued discussion. 6. Thus Western man's picture of the truth advances, by successive approximations, **closer and closer to the whole truth without ever reaching it.**
>
> This methodology of the West is basic to the success, power, and wealth of Western Civilization. It is reflected in all successful aspects of Western life, from the earliest beginnings to the

> present...Throughout Western religious history, in spite of the frequent outbursts by dissident groups insisting that the truth was available—total, explicit, final, and authoritative— in God's revelation, Western religious thought has continued to believe that revelation itself is never final, total, complete, or literal, but is a continuous symbolic process that must be interpreted and reinterpreted by discussion. The method of the West, even in religion, has been this: **The truth unfolds in time by a cooperative process of discussion that creates a temporary consensus which we hope will form successive approximations growing closer and closer to the final truth, to be reached only in some final stage of eternity.**[280]

This is the gist of their model of civilizational progress. Without denying that civilization must be built upon truth and justice, they assert that it is only possible to reach approximations of the truth through endless disputation. The discovery of truth is presented as a syncretic, collaborative process. They make no distinction between matters of religion and those of ambiguous worldly issues.[281] The above model is the essence of Western political thought. It is the common thread between conservatives and liberals.

'Conservative' and 'liberal' are merely mental constructs of the process outlined above. Meaning that anytime Western society is faced with a perplexing enigma for which paganized Christianity is ill-equipped to answer, then belief and morality are systematically loosened, thereby liberating the Westerner to do what is most 'pragmatic' and convenient. This newly adopted approach eventually becomes the traditional method that must be 'conserved' after that for posterity, until, of course, some new crisis emerges and morality and religion must be once again

---

[280] Tragedy and Hope, pp. 1228-1229.

[281] that are relegated by divine commandment to the institution of mutual consultation by qualified parties to investigate and solve.

loosened for their survival, upon which the process begins again. That is the foundation of Western thought.

The Fundamentalists

Anything divergent from this liberalist-conservative dialectic construct is considered primitive, **fundamentalist**, and narrow-minded. The 'fundamentalist' label appears to be a somewhat recent Neocon invention in its origin, seemingly invented by Bernard Lewis or one of his counterparts, from the last of the breed of old-school die-hard orientalists. It is, quite bluntly, an arbitrary blanket term applied to anyone believing in the primacy of Islam as the basis of their society, and anyone who believes in Islam as the absolute truth and arbiter in man's disputes — or in other words, whoever uncompromisingly holds fast to the core of Islam, which is belief and submission. The actual 'fundamentals' of Islam were highlighted in the second chapter of this volume. What these Western ideologues intend by it is something quite different.

At the forefront of the 'fundamentalists' whose teachings might appeal to 'traditional' Muslims, are the popularly vilified Wahhabis (a baseless, pejorative label). The da'wah of the great reformer Muḥammad b. 'Abd al Wahhāb al-Tamīmī (1115-1206h.) رَحِمَهُ ٱللَّهُ has long been the primary fascination of social scientists and their imperial overseers, a phenomenon whose precedence dates back to colonial involvement in Egypt in the early nineteenth century. The aim of these academics and those that they are beholden to is to drive a deep wedge between the 'Wahhabis' and the 'traditionalists.'

In keeping with this tradition, the contributing authors of RanD's Building Moderate Muslim Networks define the traditionalists, who they aim to rescue from 'fundamentalist' influence, as follows:

> These traditions incorporate the veneration of saints (and the offering of prayers at their tombs) and other practices that are anathema to the Wahhabis. They interpret the Islamic scriptures on the basis of the teachings of the schools of jurisprudence (mazhab) that were established in the early centuries of Islam; they do not engage in unmediated interpretation of the Quran and the hadith (the tradition of the Prophet Muhammad ﷺ), as Salafists and modernists do. Many traditionalists incorporate elements of Sufism—the tradition of Islamic mysticism that stresses emotive and personal experiences of the divine—into their practice of Islam.[282]

There is a lot to unpack in that short snippet, but in short, they focus on and exploit the main points of contention between these large bodies of Muslims, which are as follow: venerable grave-worship, gnostic mysticism, and adherence to the jurisprudence of a designated *madh'hab* regardless of whether it opposes authentic religious texts and principles. Similarly, in an earlier publication titled *The Muslim World after 9/11*, these non-Muslim self-appointed Islam-experts state:

> Traditionalists are generally conservative Muslims who uphold beliefs and traditions received and adapted through the centuries. These traditions often derive from local beliefs and practices that are not always based on orthodox Islamic

[282] Rand Corp., Building Moderate Muslim Networks, p. 73.

doctrine but over time have come to be regarded as an intrinsic part of the religion. **Traditionalism incorporates the veneration and prayers offered at the tombs of saints, belief in spirits and miracles, and the use of amulets—in short, a set of beliefs quite removed from Wahhabi severity and intolerance.** Many traditionalists incorporate aspects of Sufi beliefs and practices.[283]

The philosophical modernist 'reformist' and the mystic 'traditionalist' approaches closely resemble the Western model of loosening and tightening truth and morality to reshape and restructure religion for its social utility. In other words, their appeal is to the masses of misinformed people constituting a contentious majority who have *conserved the tradition* of incrementally *liberating Islam from its foundations* according to their whims. Anything short of that is deemed fanatical. Here again, we have the liberal-conservative paradigm of loosening and tightening, eventually secularizing revealed religion by dissolving the concept of God. In this scheme, the human mind emerges as a replacement deity, standing in as the superior arbiter in all matters of belief and morality. Thus it is more advantageous in the Western mind to merge these 'traditionalists' with the like-minded 'modernists' by all available means to thwart the so-called fundamentalists.

Fomenting a Counter-Culture Revolution in Muslim Diasporas

Lastly, their publications explicitly propose that their 'reformation' is conducted by a number of tactics. Firstly, the modernists and mainstream secularists are to be supported to sway the traditionalists—especially women and youth—to their orbit, far from 'fundamentalist' influence. Furthermore, the

[283] Rand Corp. The Muslim World after 9/11, p. 21.

'traditionalists' must be supported against the 'fundamentalists' and every effort should be made to drive a wedge between them and exacerbate disagreements, however trifling. Finally, every effort must be made to discredit those who hold a 'fundamentalist' interpretation of Islam.

This final proposal, a sustained effort to discredit the 'fundamentalist' interpretation of Islam is executed by a number of methods that are summarized as follows: 1.) Group the Salafis — those actually maintaining scriptural and doctrinal purity — with extremist terrorist groups, ranging from Shi'ite militias to the Muslim Brotherhood, al Qaeda (and more recently ISIS) and similar insurgent groups (ignoring the blatant 'modernist' and 'traditionalist' origins and constituencies of such radical political groups). 2.) Present the 'fundamentalists' as being outmoded and incapable of presenting tangible solutions for the problems of their communities, specifically those of Muslim diasporas in Western lands. 3.) Scandalize their efforts by publicizing claims of corruption or immorality in their circles — "targeting these messages especially to young people, to pious traditionalist populations, to Muslim minorities in the West, and to women." Such an organized effort neatly matches the description of the ideological attack that this first volume has elaborated upon:

> The ideological assault is a contemporary term implying the collective efforts that one nation engages in to overtake another or to cause it to redirect itself towards a specific trajectory. It is more dangerous than military attack because the ideological attack tends towards secrecy and pursuing hidden goals from its inception. Therefore, the attacked nation does not realize it, nor prepare to halt its advance or to stand against it until ultimately falling its prey. Resultantly, this nation becomes diseased in its thinking and feeling, loving what its enemy wants it to love, and hating what its enemy wants it to hate.

> It is a fatal disease that devastates nations, removing their identity, authenticity and fortitude. The nation that is afflicted by it does not feel what has stricken it or even realize it, making the remedy and the path of guidance out of it something substantially difficult. This attack takes place by means of education and culture curriculums, as well as through the media, large and small writings and other means directly related to the affairs of nations. The adversary intends behind such things to divert them from their belief and to connect them to what they promote. And we ask Allah for safety and well-being.[284]

In the second volume of this work, we further explore the direct offshoot of this age-old ideological assault. It covers over the broader discussion of the millennium-old continuum of Islamophobia stemming from the Crusades until modernity — spanning the duration of the Renaissance, the Protestant Reformation, the 'Enlightenment', colonization, until arriving on the contemporary scene where Islam is commonly conflated with regression and terror.

---

[284] Majmū' Fatāwā wa Rasā'il 'Abd al 'Azīz b. Bāz, vol. 3, p. 338. Originally published in Majallah al Buḥūth al Islāmiyyah, 8th edition, p. 286-293.

Works Consulted & Cited

Arnold, Thomas Walker. *The preaching of Islam: a history of the propagation of the Muslim faith*. Constable, (1913).

Le Bon Gustave. *Haḍarah al 'Arab* (arabic translation of La Civilization des Arabes — The Civilization of the Arabs by 'Aadil Za'īter) Hindāwī Foundation for Education and Culture (2012). [there is also a heavily summarized English rendition of this book titled: The world of Islamic civilization. Tudor Pub. Co., 1974.]

Cameron, Averil, and Stuart Hall, eds. *Eusebius' Life of Constantine*. Clarendon Press, 1999.

Cohn, Norman. *Cosmos, chaos, and the world to come: the ancient roots of apocalyptic faith.* Yale University Press, 2001.

Cohn, Norman. *The pursuit of the millennium: Revolutionary millenarians and mystical anarchists of the middle ages*. Random House, 2011.

Cornford, Francis Macdonald. *From religion to philosophy: a study in the origins of western speculation*. Courier Corporation, 2004.

Edersheim, Alfred. *The life and times of Jesus the Messiah*. Vol. 1. Longmans, Green, and Company, (1899).

Ehrman, Bart D. Lost Christianities: The battles for Scripture and the faiths we never knew. Oxford University Press, USA, 2005.

The Encyclopedia Americana, 1918-1920.

The Encyclopedia Britannica , 11th ed.

Gibb, Hamilton Alexander Rosskeen. *Modern trends in Islam*. Chicago, IL: University of Chicago Press, (1947).

Hardenbrook, V.R.F.T., *Emperor Constantine the Great (306–337)*. The Importance of His Faith in the History of the Church.

Ibn Abī-l 'Izz al Ḥanafī, Ṣadr al-Dīn Muhammad b. 'Alā' al-Dīn 'Alī b. Muhammad. *Sharḥ al 'Aqīdah al-Ṭahāwiyyah*. Taḥqīq: Ahmad Shākir. Wazārah al-Shu'ūn al Islāmiyyah wal Awqāf wal-Da'wah wal Irshād (1418 h.).

Ibn Bāz. *Majmū' Fatāwā wa Rasā'il 'Abd al 'Azīz b. Bāz*. Interview about The Ideological Assault. Originally published in Majallah al Buḥūth al Islāmiyyah, 8th edition.

Ibn Khaldūn, 'Abd al-Raḥmān b. Muhammad, Abu Zayd al Ishbīlī (808 h.). *Diwān al Mubtada' wal Khabar fī Tārīkh al 'Arab wal Barbar wa man 'Aaṣarahum min Dhawī al-Sh'an al Akbar*. Dar al Fikr, Beirut (1408/1988).

Ibn Mandah. *Kitāb al Imān*. Taḥqīq Ali b. Nāṣir al Faqīhī.. Muasasah al-Risālah, Beirut 2nd edition, (1406).

Ibn Qayyim al Jawziyyah. *Al Fawā'id*. Dar al Kutub al 'Ilmiyyah (1393/1973).

Ibn Qayyim al Jawziyyah. *Hāshiyah Ibn al Qayyim 'alā Tahdhīb al-Sunan*.

Ibn Qayyim al Jawziyyah. *'Idah al-Ṣābirīn*. Dar Ibn Kathir, Damascus, Beirut, Madinah KSA. 3rd Edition (1409/1989).

Ibn Qayyim al Jawziyyah. *Ighāthah al-Lahfān*. Maktabah al Ma'ārif, al-Riyāḍ, KSA. Tahqiq: Muhammad Hāmid al Faqī.

Ibn Qayyim al Jawziyyah. *'Ilām al Muwaqi'īn 'an Rabbil 'Alamīn*. Dar al Kutub al 'Ilmiyyah Beirut (1411).

Ibn Qayyim al Jawziyyah. *Iqtiḍā' al-Ṣirāṭ al Mustaqīm*. Dar 'Aalam al Kutub, Beirut. (1419/1999).

Ibn Qayyim al Jawziyyah. *Al Jawāb al Kāfī*. Dar al Ma'rifah, al Maghrib (1418/1997).

Ibn Qayyim al Jawziyyah. *Miftāḥ Dār al-Sa'ādah*. Dar al Kutub al 'Ilmiyyah, Beirut.

Ibn Qayyim al Jawziyyah. *Mukhtaṣar al-Sawā'iq al Mursalah 'alā al Jahmiyyah wal Mu'aṭṭilah*. Abridged by Muhammad b. Muhammad al Ba'lī (774 h.). Dar al Hadīth, Cairo (1422/2001).

Ibn Qayyim al Jawziyyah. *Rawḍah al Muḥibbīn*. Dar al Kutub al 'Ilmiyyah 1403/1983

Ibn Qayyim al Jawziyyah. *Al-Ṣalah wa hukm tārikihā*. Maktabah al-Thaqāfa, Madinah, KSA.

Ibn Qayyim al Jawziyyah. *Shifā' al 'Alīl fī Masā'il al Qaḍā' wal Qadar wal Ḥikmah wal-Ta'līl*. Dar Al Ma'rifah (1398/1978).

Ibn Qayyim al Jawziyyah. *Zād al Ma'ād fī hadi Khayr al 'Ibād*. Muassasah al-Risālah, Beirut; Maktabah al Manār al Islāmiyyah, Kuwait. 6th Edition (1415/1994).

Ibn Taymiyyah. *Dar' Ta'āruḍ al 'Aql wal-Naql*. Jāmi'ah Al Imām Muhammad b. Sa'ūd al Islāmiyyah, KSA (1411/1991).

Ibn Taymiyyah. *Al Jawāb al-Ṣaḥīḥ*. Dar al 'Aaṣimah, KSA (1419/1999).

Ibn Taymiyyah. *Majmū' al Fatāwā*. Taḥqīq: 'Abd al-Raḥmān b. Qāsim. Majma' Malik Fahd Printing Complex for the Noble Quran, Al Madinah al-Nabawiyyah, KSA. (1416/1995).

Ibn Taymiyyah. *Al-Radd 'alā al Manṭiqiyyīn*. Dār al Ma'rifah, Beirut.

James, George GM, and Molefi Kete Asante. *Stolen legacy: Greek philosophy is stolen Egyptian philosophy.* United Brothers Communications Systems, (1954).

Jongeneel, Jan AB. *Jesus Christ in world history: his presence and representation in cyclical and linear settings*. Vol. 149. Peter Lang, (2009).

Khalfullah, Muḥammad (arabic ed.) Hitti, Phillip (English ed.). Al-Thaqāfah al Islāmiyyah, wal Ḥayah al Mu'āṣirah. Maktabah al-Nahḍah al Miṣriyyah, in conjunction with Franklin Publications, New York — Cairo (1953).

Kuhn, Thomas S. *The Copernican revolution: Planetary astronomy in the development of Western thought.* Vol. 16. Harvard University Press, (1957).

al-Lālakā'ī, Abul Qāsim Hibatullah b. Al Ḥasan. *Sharḥ Usūl 'Itiqād Ahlis-Sunnah wal Jama'āh.* Taḥqīq: Ahmed b. Sa'd al Ghāmidī. Dar Tayyibah, KSA, 8th edition (1423/2003).

Maccoby, Hyam. *The mythmaker: Paul and the invention of Christianity.* Barnes & Noble Publishing, 1998.

Al Madkhalī, Rabī' b. Hādī 'Umayr. *Al-Tawhīd Awwalan* (Taken from the transcription of a lecture titled: Monotheism First; delivered in Dhul Qa'dah 1423 h. Quoted in the book *Al Mulakhaṣ al Jamīl fī Bayān Manhaj al-Shaykh Rabī' b. Hādī al Madkhalī fī al-Da'wah wal Jarḥ wal-Ta'dīl.*)

Al Madkhalī, Rabī' b. Hādī 'Umayr. *Wujūb al Ittibā' wal-Taḥdhīr min Maẓāhir al-Shirk wal-Ibtidā'.* http://rabee.net/ar/articles.php?cat=11&id=274. Retrieved June 1, 2018/ 15 Ramaḍān 1438 h.

Al Maqrīzī, Taqī al-Dīn Ahmed b. 'Alī b. 'Abd al Qādir (845 h.). Al Mawā'iẓ wal i'tibār. Dar al Kutub al 'Ilmiyyah, Beirut. 1st Edition, (1418/1998).

Al Marwazī, Muḥammad b. Naṣr al Marwazī (died 294 h.). Ta'ẓīm Qadr al-Ṣalah. Taḥqīq: Dr. 'Abd al-Raḥmān b. 'Abd al Jabbār Al Farīwā'ī; Maktabah al-Dār, Madīnah KSA. 1st edition (1406 h).

McKnight, Stephen A. "Understanding Modernity: A Reappraisal of the Gnostic Element." The Intercollegiate Review 14, no. 2 (1979): 107.

Al Mu'allimī; *Al Qā'id ilā Taṣḥīḥ al 'Aqā'id*. Al Maktab al Islāmī, 3rd Edition (1404 h./ 1984)

Pagels, Elaine. *The gnostic Paul: gnostic exegesis of the Pauline letters*. Bloomsbury Publishing USA, 1992.

Quigley, Carroll, and William Marina. *The evolution of civilizations: An introduction to historical analysis*. Indianapolis, IN (originally published in 1961): Liberty Fund, 1979.

Quigley, Carroll. *Tragedy & Hope*. New York: Macmillan, (1966).

Runia, David T. *Philo in early Christian literature: A survey*. Vol. 3. Uitgeverij Van Gorcum, 1993.

Al-Sa'dī, 'Abd al-Rahmān b. Nāṣir. *Intiṣār al Ḥaqq*

Al-Sa'dī, 'Abd al-Raḥmān b. Nāṣir. *Majmū' al Fawā'id wa Iqtināṣ al Awābid*. Dār Ibn al Jawzī (1424/2003).

Al-Sa'dī, 'Abd al-Rahmān b. Nāṣir. *Al Mukhtaṣar fī Usūl al 'Aqā'id al-Dīniyyah.*

Al-S'adī, 'Abd al-Rahmān b. Nāṣir. *Al Qawā'id al Ḥisān.*

Al-Sa'dī, 'Abd al-Raḥmān. *Risālatān fī fijnah al-Dajjāl wal Y'ajūj wal M'ajūj.* Dār ibn Al Jawzī, (2006, 2nd edition).

Al-Sa'dī, 'Abd al-Rahmān b. Nāṣir. *Tawḍīḥ al Kāfiyah al-Shāfiyah fīl Intiṣār lil Firqah al-Nājiyyah*. Dar Aḍwā' al-Salaf (1420/2000).

Al-Sa'dī, 'Abd al-Rahmān b. Nāṣir. *Taysīr al Karīm al Rahmān*. Muassasah al-Risālah (1420/2000).

Al-Sa'dī, 'Abd al-Rahmān b. Nāṣir. *Usūl 'Aẓīmah min Qawā'id al Islām*. Maktabah Dar al Minhāj (1432).

Al-Sa'dī, 'Abd al-Rahmān b. Nāṣir. *Uṣūl al-Dīn*

Smith, Wilfred Cantwell. *Islam in modern history*. Vol. 268. Signet, (1959).

Stoddard, Lothrop. *The new world of Islam.* New York: C. Scribner's Sons, (1921).

Tuggy, Dale, *"Trinity", The Stanford Encyclopedia of Philosophy* (Winter 2016 Edition), Edward N. Zalta (ed.), URL = <https://plato.stanford.edu/archives/win2016/entries/trinity/>.

Vail, Charles H. *Ancient Mysteries and Modern Masonry*. New York City, N.Y. : Macoy Publishing and Masonic Supply Co., (1909).

Voegelin, Eric. *Science, politics and gnosticism*: Two essays. Regnery Publishing, 2012.

Volney, Constantin-François. *The Ruins, or, a Survey of the Revolutions of Empires.* Joseph Mann & Company, 1823.

van den Broek, Roelof, and Wouter J. Hanegraaff, eds. *Gnosis and hermeticism from antiquity to modern times*. SUNY Press, 1998.

Young, Theodore Cuyler. *Near Eastern Culture and Society*. Princeton University Press, 2017.

Notes:

Notes:

Notes:

Notes:

Made in the USA
Monee, IL
13 January 2022

88817732R00135